EDITOR: MARTIN W WINDROW

W9-AYN-439

OSPREY
MILITARY

MEN-AT-ARMS SERIES   156

THE ROYAL MARINES 1956-84

Text by
WILLIAM FOWLER
Colour plates by
PAUL HANNON

First published in Great Britain in 1984 by
Osprey Publishing, Elms Court,
Chapel Way, Botley, Oxford OX2 9LP
United Kingdom

© Copyright 1984 Osprey Publishing Ltd.
Reprinted 1985, 1987 (twice), 1989, 1991, 1994,
1995, 1998

British Library Cataloguing in Publication Data

Fowler, William,
  The Royal Marines 1956–84—(Men at Arms
  series; 156)
  1. Great Britain. *Royal Marines*—History—20th
  century
  I. Title   II. Series
  359.9'6'0941   VE57

  ISBN 0-85045-568-5

Filmset in Great Britain
Printed through World Print Ltd, Hong Kong

FOR A CATALOGUE OF ALL BOOKS PUBLISHED BY
OSPREY MILITARY, AUTOMOTIVE AND AVIATION PLEASE WRITE TO:

**The Marketing Manager
Osprey Publishing Ltd., PO Box 140
Wellingborough, Northants NN8 4ZA
United Kingdom**

Author's Note:

My thanks to the Royal Marines PR Office in
Whitehall; the Commando Forces News Team,
Plymouth; the Royal Marines Museum, Eastney; the
Ministry of Defence; and the Royal United Services
Institute. I am grateful to James Ladd, who
introduced me to the Corps in 1982, and whose book
The Royal Marines 1919–1980 is an excellent authorised
history; and to Les Scriver, for access to his unique
photographic record of today's Corps. Thanks to the
many men of the Royal Marines, especially in 3
Commando Brigade RM, who gave me their time
and patience in some testing and trying places.

   This book is dedicated to VH and SP, to whom I
will always be a 'Percy Pongo'.

The Royal Marines 1956-84

Introduction

A *Punch* cartoon of the 1920s shows a Royal Marine aboard a warship pulling on his tunic, with the caption: 'A Handy Man. Marine (somewhat late for parade): "At six o'clock I was a bloomin' 'ousemaid; at seven o'clock I was a bloomin' valet; at eight o'clock I was a bloomin' waiter; and *now* I'm a bloomin' soldier!"' He could reasonably have added that he was also expected to crew naval guns, take part in boarding parties, and fight his way ashore on landing and 'cutting-out' expeditions, without exhausting the list of tasks which the Royal Marine was called upon to perform before the Second World War.

The housemaid, valet and waiter are things of the past; but in the last quarter of the 20th century the Royal Marine remains a serviceman who combines the skills of seafarer and soldier. As the author can vouch, from the men he has talked with in the jungle, in the Arctic, and in barracks, the Corps produces a truly 'handy man'.

Suggest to a Royal Marine that he is some kind of 'soldier', and his reaction will be one of disgust, or worse: he is jealous of his special identity. For a start, his physical entry standards are higher than those of the Army. The Commando training embraces all the men in 3 Commando Brigade, and sets a common standard for the Brigadier and colonels, the technicians of the Commando Logistic Regiment, and the section commander and 'booty' at the 'sharp end'. In the author's observation the Corps attracts a highly motivated and intelligent recruit; to pass the Commando course as well as to learn a wide variety of modern military skills demands a well-balanced mix of brains and beef. Like any force that attracts this type of man, once it has tested and trained him the Corps accepts him into a close-knit and self-confident family.

As a 'Special Forces' organisation the Royal Marines and their supporting Commando-trained arms are unique. Other special forces trace their origins only to the Second World War; but the Royal Marines date back to 1664, when the Duke of York and Albany's Maritime Regiment of Foot was raised to serve aboard Royal Navy warships. A chequered history during the 17th and 18th centuries included service by maritime units right across the world, from the Americas to Australia, on board ship and ashore. In the wars with France between the 1790s and 1815 they served aboard as gun crews, as landing and boarding parties, and as sharpshooters.

No complete list of the Royal Marines' memorable actions over more than three centuries of global service is possible in a book of this kind; but a few of the most famous may be mentioned. The only battle-honour actually displayed by the Corps is 'Gibraltar', which traditionally stands to repre-

Marines of 45 Commando RM aboard a Westland Whirlwind helicopter on the carrier HMS *Theseus* before taking off for Port Said, 6 November 1956. The man in the centre has a folded 3.5in. rocket launcher, the rest Lee Enfield No.4 Mk.1 rifles.
(Most of the photos in this book are reproduced by courtesy of the RM Historical Photo Library/RM Museum, RM Eastney, Southsea, Hampshire, where the assistance of Mr. Harry Playford was invaluable to the author. Where known, photographers are named, e.g. the prolific and highly skilled Pete Holdgate.)

Off Port Said, 6 November 1956: a stick of Royal Marines of 45 Cdo. scramble aboard a Whirlwind on the flight deck of *Theseus* on their way to the first helicopter assault in the history of airmobile operations.

their honour no other 4th Bn. has ever been raised since.

The Corps served all over the world during the Second World War, but a particularly notable action was fought on the same coast as the Zeebrugge raid—at Walcheren, one of the strongly defended Scheldt estuary islands covering the approaches to the vital port of Antwerp. In a complex operation, supported by RAF Lancaster bombers and by tracked amphibious vehicles, 4 Cdo.Bde. landed 41, 47 and 48 RM Cdos. on

sent all the others. It commemorates the capture of the Rock from the Spanish during the war with Spain and France in the early years of the 18th century. In July 1704 some 1,900 British and 40 Dutch Marines landed and captured the position, which they then defended successfully during a nine-month siege.

In 1761 Marines mounted a cross-Channel attack against the coast of Brittany, establishing a cliff-top beachhead at Belle Isle by the exercise of climbing skills which are still much in evidence in today's Corps.

Some 2,700 Royal Marines ('Royal' since 1802) were embarked on the Royal Navy warships which defeated the Franco-Spanish fleet at Trafalgar on 21 October 1805; Capt. Adair, RM commanded 40 of them on the quarterdeck and poop of the flagship HMS *Victory*, where Admiral Lord Nelson fell, and in all the Royal Marine detachments suffered 342 killed.

Among many First World War actions the cross-Channel raid against the German submarine base at Zeebrugge in Belgium on 23 April 1918—St George's Day—was probably the most famous. HMS *Vindictive* and her accompanying ferries were raked by enemy batteries even before they could come alongside Zeebrugge mole; but in fierce fighting the men of the 4th RM Bn. secured the area, allowing block-ships to be sunk in the approaches to the port. The 4th Bn. suffered 366 casualties out of a strength of 703 all ranks; and in

Glossary

AWT	...Arctic Warfare Trained
BARV	...Beach Armoured Recovery Vehicle
Bde	...Brigade
BMA	...Brigade Maintenance Area
Cdo	...Commando
CGRM	...Commandant General Royal Marines
CO	...Commanding Officer
Coy	...Company
CTC	...Commando Training Centre
FAA	...Fleet Air Arm
GPMG	...General Purpose Machine Gun
LCA	...Landing Craft, Assault
LCU	...Landing Craft, Utility
LCVP	...Landing Craft, Vehicle/Personnel
LMG	...Light Machine Gun
LPD	...Landing Platform Dock
LSL	...Landing Ship, Logistic
LST	...Landing Ship, Tank
LVT	...Landing Vehicle, Tracked
LZ	...Landing Zone
M&AW	...Mountain & Arctic Warfare
ML	...Mountain Leader
NBC	...Nuclear, Biological & Chemical
RCL	...Ramp Cargo Lighter
RMBPD	...Royal Marine Boom Patrol Detachment
RTR	...Royal Tank Regiment
SAS	...Special Air Service
SBS	...Special Boat Squadron
SC	...Swimmer/Canoeist
SLR	...Self-Loading Rifle
Sqn	...Squadron
Tp	...Troop
USMC	...United States Marine Corps

Westkapelle on 1 November 1944, while No.4 Army Commando attacked Flushing.

On an individual basis, Commandos remember Dieppe, 19 August 1942 (40 Cdo.); Salerno, 9 September 1943 (41 Cdo.); Kangaw in the Arakan, 31 January 1945 (42 Cdo.); and Montforterbeek, 23 January 1945 (45 Cdo.). The assault and raiding squadrons brought men and equipment ashore on D-Day, 6 June 1944; and 'Comacchio' Gp., now tasked with the protection of North Sea oil rigs, recalls in its title the action fought in northern Italy in April 1945 when 2 Cdo.Bde. (2, 9, 40 and 43 Cdos.) broke through German lines around Lake Comacchio—an action during which Cpl. Tom Hunter won a posthumous VC. The Corps have won ten VCs in all, five of them during the First World War, but the first as long ago as 1854, when Cpl. John Prettyjohns led a section against Russians defending cave positions at Inkerman in the Crimea.

The Royal Marines as they are known today owe their origin to the Second World War. Marines fulfilled many rôles between 1939 and 1945, serving as gun crews aboard warships, coxswains for landing craft, and even as crews for specialist armoured vehicles. The Commando rôle was born of the decision to mount vigorous raiding operations against Occupied Europe, a decision taken as soon as it became clear that British conventional forces would be forced to withdraw from France in 1940. Special forces would be required for these operations; and Lt.Col. Dudley Clarke, Military Assistant to Sir John Dill, the CIGS in June 1940, suggested that they be called 'Commandos', after the Boer irregulars who had operated behind British lines in the South African War. During the war Commandos—the term being used both for the troops, and for the battalion-sized unit—were raised from both the Army and the Royal Marines; by late 1942 as many as 79 Army regiments and corps were represented. It was at that time that the famous green beret was introduced for Commando forces. After the war the Army units were disbanded. The Royal Marine Commandos were retained, as was the tough course which all officers and men have to pass before they can wear the green beret. The Corps kept up all the historical traditions of the Royal Marines of bygone generations, including their dress uniforms, military music, and many barracks and bases.

The Royal Marine Commandos have been in action almost without a break since 1946. In 1948 they covered the withdrawal from Palestine. In 1950–52 they were engaged in anti-terrorist operations during the Malayan Emergency, and fought alongside US Marines in Korea. In 1953–54 they were involved in internal security duties in the Suez Canal Zone, and two years later the Commando Brigade returned to Egypt in Operation 'Musketeer', the Anglo-French landings at Port Said. In 1955–59 Marines operated against EOKA terrorists in Cyprus. In 1960 the first Commando Carrier was commissioned. Between 1960 and 1967 Commandos served in Aden, fighting in the Radfan Mts. and covering the final British withdrawal; and also saw action in Borneo and western Malaysia during the 'Confrontation' with Indonesia. There were additional operational deployments to Kuwait in 1961, and East Africa in 1964. From 1969 to the present day the 'Royal' has shared the soldier's burden in Northern Ireland. In 1982 3 Cdo.Bde. sailed south to the Falklands, and carried out the planning for Operation 'Sutton', the landings and subsequent advance on East Falkland, during which the Royal Marines

A patrol of Z Troop, 45 Cdo. RM move through streets damaged by shellfire after the fighting ceased in Port Said. They wear Denison smocks; the left hand man has an Energa anti-tank grenade tied to the back of his belt; and in front of him the Bren No.2 has the LMG spare parts wallet slung across his back.

provided three of the eight battalions employed in the infantry rôle, apart from specialist supporting units.

The events between Operations 'Musketeer' and 'Sutton' spanned only 26 years, and several 'Royals' served in both. Lt. G. H. Jackson, QM of 3 Cdo.Bde. Air Sqn. in 1982, was Mne. Jackson of Y Tp., 42 Cdo. at Suez. Lt. Col. N. F. Vaux commanded 42 Cdo. in the Falklands; he was 2nd Lt. Vaux of X Tp., 45 Cdo. in 1956. Lt. B. J. Bellas, MTO of 45 Cdo. in 1982, was Cpl. Bellas of A Tp., 40 Cdo. in 1956. In 1982 the Chaplain to the Commando Forces was the Rev. Peter Gregson— who had been a Marine (S3) with 42 Cdo. during Britain's last major amphibious operation. On board the SS *Canberra* when she sailed to the South Atlantic was Mne. Tom Powers of 40 Cdo. QM staff; in 1956 he had been with HMS *Newfoundland*'s RM detachment—but he did not get on shore in either operation! These veterans of a quarter-century of Royal Marine history would testify that the years between have been both busy and challenging.

Suez, 1956

On 26 July 1956 President Gamel Abdul Nasser of Egypt seized the Suez Canal from the Anglo-French company which administered it. After the failure of various political moves the military option, Operation 'Musketeer', was developed with the French. A delay allowed 40 and 42 Cdos. to train with C Sqn., 6th RTR, whose Centurion tanks had been waterproofed for a landing alongside 40 Commando.

The most interesting development was the preserve of 45 Commando. An experimental Army/RAF helicopter squadron with six Whirlwind Mk.2 and six Sycamore Mk.14 were joined by the eight Whirlwinds of 845 FAA Sqn.; and this (for those days) not inconsiderable helicopter lift was to carry 45 Cdo. into battle in the first recorded assault helicopter operation in land warfare, in the sense of a significant troop landing into the battle area.

The seaborne assault involved three LSTs (Assault), five LSTs and eight LCTs. The RTR had provided drivers for a troop of 16 tracked

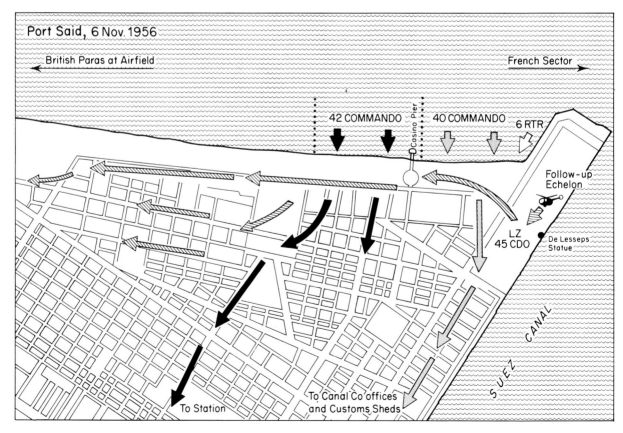

LVTs, though one vehicle had to be cannibalised for spares. 45 Cdo. embarked aboard the carriers HMS *Ocean* and *Theseus*, where they had an opportunity to practise helicopter drills and to develop the now-universal tactic of the 'stick'—the group of men carried by one helicopter.

The morning of 6 November ('L-Day', since 'D-Day' was felt to be a politically sensitive phrase) dawned hazy. Fires started by air strikes and naval gunfire left long stains of smoke across the sky above Port Said. The two Commandos made their assault in waves, with the leading wave of two troops in LVTs and a second wave in LCAs. 40 Cdo. landed at the base of the western mole at the entrance to the Suez Canal, with the Royal Tank Regiment tucked in on their left. 42 Cdo. was on their right, with the Casino Pier as a clear landmark dividing the two beachheads. A Naval Gunfire observer in the first wave watched as a fellow-NGFO called down 4in. shells on the Casino; as it disappeared under the smoke and dust he cheerfully signalled back to his opposite number: 'Every one a coconut!'

The LVTs passed through the line of wooden chalets which bordered the shore and made for the line of houses which was their first objective. The Centurion tanks came ashore at the Fisherman's Harbour at H + 90, 15 minutes after the first wave; in company with 40 Cdo., they moved off along the streets bordering the western bank of the Canal. Their objectives were the harbour basins which would be used for landing reinforcements from II Corps.

Officers of HQ, 45 Cdo. RM confer during Operation 'Lucky Alphonse' on Cyprus, 1956. They wear Denison smocks; and the blackened webbing which characterised Royal Marines from 1948.

The advance was begun by P Tp., with Y Tp. passing through them. When B Tp. took over the Egyptian resistance had begun to stiffen; two officers, Lts. McCarthy and Ufton, were killed while leading their men in the unpleasant business of house-clearing. By the end of the day 40 Cdo. had reached the customs sheds and Canal Company offices; the Centurions blasted holes in the buildings before they were cleared.

While 40 Cdo. were fighting down the Canal, 42 Cdo. had sent A Tp., together with a tank, to rescue the British Consul. There was some talk of a ceasefire when 40 Cdo. Mortar Officer produced the Egyptian brigadier commanding the garrison; however, the prospect receded when it became clear that this officer had little contact with or control over the local forces.

42 Cdo. had a hair-raising drive down open roads flanked by tall buildings. Lt. Peter Mayo, a

An RM Commando with a Sten Mk.V SMG guards a dejected group of Egyptian officers, ratings and soldiers during the Suez operation.

While certainly posed, this photo of Royal Marines checking a hut near Akanthou, Cyprus during Operation 'Turkey Trot', 1956, does give some idea of the typical scene. They wear summer shirtsleeve order, and carry the No.4 Mk.1 rifle, the Sten Mk.V SMG, and the Browning 9mm pistol. (Keystone)

National Service officer, recalled that his LVT was slower than the others; as it fell behind, it came under increasingly heavy fire. The RTR driver was hit by a .50cal. round and died in the young officer's arms; Mayo himself narrowly escaped severe wounds when small arms fire creased his arms and grenade fragments sliced open a chunk of scalp and 'started a much-needed haircut'. Fire from Egyptians was hard to locate at times, since some were dressed in civilian-style *galabia* robes. With military delicacy the Marines of 42 Cdo. drew a distinction between 'wogs'—who were armed—and 'civvies'—who weren't.

42 Cdo. had moved out from the beachhead at about 0930 hrs, with a tank leading, followed by the LVT of B Tp. commander. Tanks were mixed in with A and X Tps., the machine gun sections and Coy. Tac. HQ. Their objectives were the Nile Cold Storage Co. Plant, and the Power Station. The LVTs were not fitted with armour plates, since they had been loaded at Malta for an 'exercise' as part of the cover plan for 'Musketeer'. Even so, only one LVT was knocked out during the run to the Power Station. At the close of the day the Marines began to make themselves at home in their objectives, and to set out defences. Lt. Mayo recalled the chalked names that appeared, including 'Shag's Shack' and 'Home Sweet Holmes'. He noted in his diary: 'The subtopian effect is given by "Mrs & Mrs Brown—The Nest".'

45 Cdo. were due to land at H + 55 minutes; but when the CO, Lt.Col. Norman Tailyour, made a recce flight to check the proposed LZ it was obscured by smoke, and the pilot landed at the sports stadium. The Whirlwind returned quickly after seeing 'the Egyptian Army coming over the surrounding walls', and the HQ staff were lifted to safety. They selected an LZ by the statue of De Lesseps on the western breakwater. Ten minutes later the helicopters flew in, with Sycamores and Whirlwinds from *Ocean* making an orbit to the left and Whirlwinds from *Theseus* one to the right. At three-minute intervals they hovered about a foot from the ground to unload their troops. The men of 45 Cdo. had flown in with a considerable load of ammunition and weapons; those who sat inside the Sycamores had mortar and anti-tank ammunition dumped in their laps 'to act as an anchor' for Marines hanging on to them on each side with their legs dangling out the door! The assault was made in four waves; thereafter the helicopters worked as an airborne ferry service to move ammunition and stores—a task which would be repeated 26 years later in the Falklands.

As 45 Cdo. 'shook out' to clear the town of Suez towards Gamil airport (held by men of the Parachute Regt.), a Fleet Air Arm Wyvern fighter-bomber strafed the HQ party, killing one Marine and wounding 15 others including the CO and his Intelligence Officer. The same aircraft then proceeded to attack 3 Cdo.Bde. HQ under Brig. R. W. Madoc; and went on to make a pass at 42 Commando. The error was caused by an incorrect map grid reference given by the Joint Fire Support Control Committee, who were at that time still afloat.

The men of 45 Cdo. worked across the town, and it was not until the evening that they joined up with 3 Para: although Egyptian resistance was uncoordinated, it was hard to root out the snipers from the arcades and side streets.

At the close of the day the FAA were called in by 40 Cdo. to attack Navy House—the former Royal Navy headquarters in Port Said. It was pulverised by rockets and set alight, and yielded 20 prisoners and 30 enemy dead. The fighting around Navy House was the fiercest the Marines experienced that day. By nightfall the Bde. HQ was ashore and installed in two blocks of flats on the seafront, with the three Commandos deployed over a three-mile radius.

With the declaration of the ceasefire, the Commandos were ordered to return fire only if they were attacked. Even so, they conducted searches, and in the shanty town area controlled by 45 Cdo. they found 57 three-ton truckloads of arms and ammunition.

By L + 8 the Bde. HQ, 40 and 45 Cdo. had been withdrawn to Malta, while 42 Cdo. served on under 19 Bde. until relieved by Norwegians of the United Nations Force. The Bde. had suffered nine fatalities and 60 wounded, and received six gallantry decorations. The CGRM, Gen. Sir Campbell Hardy, had made a thoroughly unofficial visit during 45 Cdo.'s landing operation, on the grounds that 'over a third of the Corps were at Suez'.

HMS Newfoundland

Patrolling in the Red Sea to the south, HMS *Newfoundland* had fought the only naval action of the campaign. The Royal Navy cruiser had encountered the Egyptian frigate *Domiat*, and signalled her to heave to. The Egyptian captain ignored this instruction, and as the *Newfoundland* closed to 1,500 yards the order was given to open fire. Despite the heavy weight of fire from the British warship, the Egyptians bravely returned fire until their vessel capsized. Aboard the *Newfoundland* Royal Marines had served 6in. guns—the last time RM crews would serve naval guns in anger. B/Sgt. Evans and Mne. Waite were among those wounded by two 4in. hits from the Egyptian frigate.

Cyprus, Aden and the Persian Gulf

Hunting EOKA

While the world was distracted by Suez, the Hungarian Uprising and France's war in Algeria, the British were still enmeshed with the Greek-led EOKA movement in Cyprus. Committed to taking the island, with its divided and mutually hostile population of Greeks and Turks, into a full union with Greece, EOKA waged a low-level war of murder, ambush, and bombing. In retrospect the casualty figures and the level of destruction suffered

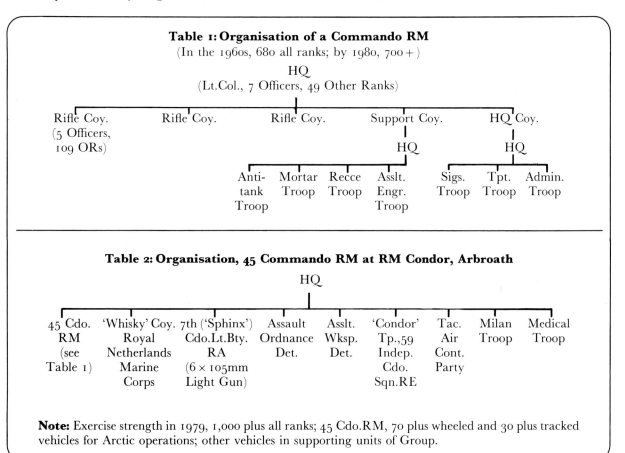

Table 1: Organisation of a Commando RM
(In the 1960s, 680 all ranks; by 1980, 700+)
HQ
(Lt.Col., 7 Officers, 49 Other Ranks)

Rifle Coy. (5 Officers, 109 ORs)	Rifle Coy.	Rifle Coy.	Support Coy. HQ	HQ Coy. HQ
			Anti-tank Troop — Mortar Troop — Recce Troop — Asslt. Engr. Troop	Sigs. Troop — Tpt. Troop — Admin. Troop

Table 2: Organisation, 45 Commando RM at RM Condor, Arbroath
HQ

45 Cdo. RM (see Table 1)	'Whisky' Coy. Royal Netherlands Marine Corps	7th ('Sphinx') Cdo.Lt.Bty. RA (6 × 105mm Light Gun)	Assault Ordnance Det.	Asslt. Wksp. Det.	'Condor' Tp.,59 Indep. Cdo. Sqn.RE	Tac. Air Cont. Party	Milan Troop	Medical Troop

Note: Exercise strength in 1979, 1,000 plus all ranks; 45 Cdo.RM, 70 plus wheeled and 30 plus tracked vehicles for Arctic operations; other vehicles in supporting units of Group.

September 1979—a very different kind of operation on Cyprus is marked by the presentation of United Nations Medals at UNFICYP BRITCON Base. The Colours of 41 Commando RM are paraded by (left to right) Lt. M. Bailey, C/Sgt. A. Higgins, WO2 R. Williams, C/Sgt. W. Newton, Lt. A. Airey. All wear light khaki drill tropical shirts and slacks with the pale blue UN Forces beret and cravat. The UN badge is worn on the upper left arm above a small Union flag patch; the yellow 41 Cdo. lanyard can just be made out on the right shoulder, and (Lt. Bailey) the dark blue officer's lanyard on the left.

at various times over the next three years. Always innovative, they set up joint military/police headquarters; and Maj. Ian De'ath, 2IC of 45 Cdo., ran a military/police training course at Nicosia. In riot control, the Marines abandoned the clumsy mix of riot shields, helmets and batons for fast-moving teams clad in gym-shoes for agility. Lt. P. Montgomery trained dogs for tracking, and led long patrols on the trail of the elusive terrorist bands. (Dogs would later be used again for tracking in Malaya and Borneo during the 'Confrontation'.)

The Commandos earned an interesting compliment from the EOKA leader 'General' Grivas, who remarked on the thoroughness of their searches. Men would be lowered into deep wells, and would patiently sift through refuse in farmyards. In one instance they located arms and ammunition hidden in a monastery. In February 1956, when weather conditions were so severe that two men died of exposure in a broken-down truck, 45 Cdo. carried out the testing task of delivering explosives to mines

Mne. Limmer of 41 Cdo. checking a shepherd during a UN tour on Cyprus between May and November 1979. He wears the DPM tropical shirt/jacket, OG trousers, and the UN beret; a first field dressing is taped to the side of his '58-pattern belt order.

in Cyprus seem somewhat modest; at the time, they absorbed considerable British energy and military resources. Their impact on the British public can perhaps be understood better if we reflect that to the generation of the mid-1950s the costlier and gaudier horrors of Ulster were an unsuspected nightmare. It was EOKA who first introduced the British newspaper reader to such novel forms of warfare as murdering soldiers' wives during shopping expeditions; and was assured of undivided attention, in consequence.

On 6 September 1955, with the situation deteriorating, 45 Cdo. deployed to Cyprus. By 0900 hrs on 10 September some 1,300 Marines were ashore with 150 vehicles, and elements were sent into the Kyrenia Mountains.

Different Commandos were on duty in the island

in the region. That winter men of the Commando's X Tp. operated on skis. In May 1957 40 Cdo. took over from 45; under Lt.Col. Jack Richards, the men of 40 used the Whirlwind helicopters of RN 728 (Cdo.) Flight to develop airmobile patrol techniques.

During their operational tours on Cyprus the Royal Marines lost a total of 10 dead. The Corps would return to the troubled island in future years, this time in a more peaceful rôle as part of the United Nations Peace-Keeping Force which stood between the two ethnic communities.

Commando Carriers

In 1960 the Royal Marines placed 42 Cdo. aboard HMS *Bulwark* (23,300 tons), the first Royal Navy carrier converted into a Commando ship. With its own 'organic' complement of helicopters, the Commando Carrier formed a mobile base capable of deploying a battalion-sized infantry unit and its vehicles, with attached Royal Artillery and Royal Engineers. The Group could be landed by helicopter in two hours, and supplied on shore from the resources of the carrier. HMS *Albion* soon joined 'the rusty B' in this rôle; and during the 1960s one carrier was normally stationed in the Mediterranean and the other in the Far East. The Commando Carriers were born of the National Defence Review of 1957, which also led to the re-activation of 41 and 43 Cdos. in 1960 and 1961 respectively.

Aden and the Gulf

The Colony and town of Aden presented the Royal Marines with a mixed environment of Arab town and harsh desert mountains. In April 1960, 45 Cdo. deployed to this unattractive but strategically important colony. Not long afterwards, at the northern end of the Persian Gulf, the tiny state of Kuwait was threatened by its larger neighbour, Iraq. 42 Cdo., under Lt.Col. E. R. Bridges, had been working up their new drills and skills aboard HMS *Bulwark*; and 14 months after 45 arrived in Aden, both units were sent deep into the Persian Gulf to protect Sheikh Abdulla and his newly-independent state.

The first wave of *Bulwark*'s Commandos arrived by helicopter on the partially-constructed airfield. The RAF Hunter jets which joined them there

'Casevac' from the desert hills of the Aden back-country: Capt. Brind, of 45 Cdo. RM, is prepared for lifting out by Scout helicopter after being wounded on 26 May 1964. Marines, and Navy helicopter personnel, wear typically informal desert dress, including the huge 'Bombay Bloomer' shorts, and suede 'brothel creepers'.

found a small local sandstorm created by the Whirlwinds as they deplaned men and equipment. 45 Cdo., under Lt.Col. L. G. Marsh, added to the traffic when they flew in from Aden in a mixture of Britannia, Beverley and Hastings fixed-wing transports. The two Commandos were quickly deployed to their main positions two miles south-east of the main road from Iraq—one of the hottest places on earth in mid-summer. By 5 July the Iraqis were reported to be building defences, and the prospect of an attack by two of their armoured regiments receded. On 21 July 42 Cdo. re-embarked on *Bulwark*; 45 Cdo. had returned to Aden on the 19th. The operation had only involved three weeks' duty, but in an extremely harsh climate and at very short notice—the first elements of 42 Cdo. had touched down within 24 hours of the Sheikh's appeal to Britain, and 45 Cdo. had moved 1,600 miles in a day, with only a brief stopover at Bahrain. Such prompt deployment had served notice of intent on Gen. Kassem's Iraqi regime, and no attack materialised.

A bomb attack on the High Commissioner on 10 December 1963 put Aden back into the news. From then onwards the campaign there fell into two distinct phases: internal security operations in Aden town, where two rival insurgent organisations called FLOSY and the NLF fought it out in the streets; and more conventional operations against tribesmen in the mountainous northern border area

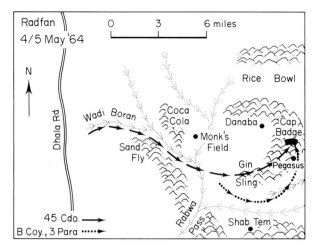

Radfan
4/5 May '64

0   3   6 miles

N

Dhala Rd

Wadi Boran

Coca Cola

Rice   Bowl

Sand Fly

Monk's Field

Danaba

Cap Badge

Gin Sling

Pegasus

Rabwa Pass

Shab Tem

45 Cdo. ——►
B Coy., 3 Para ·····►

of the Radfan.

The Radfan was a punishingly desolate region of some 400 square milies. Tribes on the Yemeni border felt free to exact tolls from convoys and travellers moving between the Western Aden Protectorate and the Yemen, and were encouraged in these depredations by the now-Marxist state to the north. Operations aimed at re-asserting authority, and showing the Egyptian-backed tribesmen that free passage would be enforced, sent British and Federal Regular Army troops deep into the harsh mountains, especially the area east of the road to Dhala.

In 1964 45 Cdo. were attached to the temporarily-named 'Radforce' for part of Operation 'Nutcracker', and men of B Coy., 3 Para were put under command. On the night of 30 April, 45 Cdo. made a night march to a high feature seven miles east of the Dhala Road, above a valley nicknamed 'Rice Bowl'. There was planned to be an airborne landing by B Coy., 3 Para on a feature called 'Cap Badge' south-east of 'Rice Bowl'; but casualties suffered by the SAS patrol that had been tasked with marking and securing the DZ led Brig. Hargroves, the Army Force Commander, to cancel it. In a rapid re-evaluation of the operation, Maj. Mike Banks of 45 Cdo. decided that he could lead his company up a steep climb to 'Coca Cola', a 1,500ft ridge about three miles east of the Dhala Road. The Commando's X and Y Coys. made this climb using 'a rather tatty length of manilla rope' which the major had brought along 'just in case . . .' Z Coy. occupied 'Sand Fly', another feature south of 'Coca Cola'.

After five full days in their positions, the Marines received orders for a night attack on 'Cap Badge'. They moved south of the Danaba basin, and hooked to their left through the ridge feature called 'Gin Sling'. At first light B Coy., 3 Para were in an exposed position on the eastern slope of 'Cap Badge' and under accurate fire. Z Coy., 45 Cdo. flew in by helicopter, and strikes by RAF Hunters finally drove the opposition off at about 1500 hours.

45 Cdo. were to operate in the area on and off for the next few months. Two men of X Coy. were wounded when the company, under command of 3 Para, came under heavy fire from six LMGs at Wadi Dhubsan. On 26 May the CO of 3 Para, Lt.Col. Farrar-Hockley, was rescued by Marines when his helicopter was forced to land near Z Coy. positions after being damaged by small arms fire during a recce flight.

There were patrols and ambushes throughout July, August and September of 1964. In 1965, as part of Operation 'Cut', patrols attacked an enemy position in the north of the Radfan about six miles east of Dhala; the position was cleared after a fire-fight and an air strike. Patrolling continued; in one two-month period the Commando completed 305 major patrols, and in 1966 some sniping incidents

In contrast, these Marines on Internal Security patrol in Aden town during 1966 wear 'pusser's order': neat shirts, shorts, long socks, berets, and weapons secured to the wrist with the sling—a familiar sight in recent years in Ulster.

In the blinding heat and choking dust of the Radfan, X Coy., 45 Cdo. RM prepare to hit the road back to base after an operation in the desert. In the foreground, a radio operator 'nets in' his A41 man-pack set.

led to long-range fire-fights. In the rundown to withdrawal in 1967 the Marines were kept busy with patrols and road-security work.

The port of Aden, meanwhile, had its own troubles, and 45 Cdo. were redeployed there into a warren of back streets. Grenades and sniping made patrols hazardous. One alert young Marine spotted a package flying from a window, shouted '*Grenade!*', and put a round through the offending window. A very frightened Arab was then arrested, but only for littering—he had just thrown away the wrapping from his midday meal.

On 11 October HMS *Albion* arrived in Aden with 42 Cdo. on board. Fresh from the Far East, and still in olive green uniforms, they took up positions in the 'Pennine Chain' (the ridge line to the north of the port and airfield) and sealed it off from the rocket and mortar attacks mounted by FLOSY and the NLF. 42 Cdo. had the tragic distinction of suffering the last casualty in Aden when their positions came under fire on 11 November 1967. The British withdrawal from Aden took place at the end of that month; 45 Cdo. were lifted out by Hercules on 28 November, and 42 Cdo. left on the 29th. The Royal

Marine landing craft hand who cast off from the harbour quay was probably the last British serviceman to leave Aden.

There was an additional Royal Marine presence in the Middle East and Gulf from 1957, when a detachment was put ashore to assist the Sultan of Muscat and Oman. Tribes incited by the Imam Ghabia and assisted by Saudi money and Egyptian propaganda waged a small-scale war against the sultan. In December 1957 a lieutenant and six NCOs were landed, drawn from ship detachments in the Persian Gulf Frigate Squadron; they were joined by other officers and NCOs from the Commando Bde. on six-month tours. The officers commanded companies, and the SNCOs platoons, of the sultan's Baluchi and Omani troops. This was a war fought with modest resources, but was a useful training-ground for junior leaders. By mid-1959 20 officers and 63 NCOs had served in Oman; two NCOs had been killed in action. These secondments ceased in 1976.

A more remarkable presence was the small training team sent to Iran in the last months of the Shah's reign in the 1970s. They were faced with the daunting task of training a Commando (others were envisaged), and of establishing a Commando school. This ambitious project was later expanded; and by February 1979 some 1,500 Iranian Commandos had been almost completely trained at their base at Manjil, while at Bushire on the Gulf a Commando HQ, three rifle companies and a support company were 70 per cent trained. The Islamic revolution of the Ayatollah Khomeini brought the programme to an end, and the Iranian Marines rallied to the new regime.

Confrontation in the Far East

While 45 Cdo. was involved in Britain's withdrawal from 'East of Suez', the Corps was also heavily committed to a campaign which proved a high-spot of Britain's post-colonial operations.

The landscape of Aden speaks for itself in this photo of a patrol from 7 Tp., Z Coy., 45 Cdo. RM in the Radfan Mountains in 1963. Section commander, Cpl. Dorling; GPMG gunner, Mne. Goffett; GPMG No.2, Mne. Gibson; rifleman, Mne. Sykes; 3.5in. RL, Mne. Allen.

At the beginning of the 1960s the showpiece of Britain's relatively peaceful and harmonious shedding of her Empire was the newly-independent Federation of Malaysia, comprising Malaya, Singapore, Sabah and Sarawak. Bordered on land and sea by Indonesia, Malaysia was seen by the ambitious and forceful Indonesian leader President Sukarno both as an economic threat, and as offering territories ripe for inclusion in the Indonesian sphere of influence. More simply, Sukarno vowed to 'smash Malaysia'. Britain's continuing treaty obligations to the new federation brought all her armed services into 'confrontation' with Indonesia—the euphemism for what was in fact a jungle war.

Limbang

The curtain-raiser to this campaign took place in the tiny oil- and gas-rich state of Brunei; though not

December 1962: a Ramp Loading Lighter carrying men of L Coy., 42 Cdo. RM back from their successful rescue mission to Limbang approaches a jetty at Brunei Town.

when on patrol. Royal Navy pilots continued to enjoy an excellent reputation for flying in poor weather and visibility to remote and hazardous LZs to extract men who had been patrolling in one of the most fatiguing climates in the world. 'Roping down'—climbing down a rope from a hovering helicopter—reduced the need to locate or prepare a large landing zone.

In some areas sand-bagged positions were built close to the Indonesian border, and used as a base for patrols. From these bases the Marines were able to intercept Indonesians as they withdrew after incursions into Malaysia. Rats infested these jungle 'keeps' in huge numbers. One quartermaster was informed that the quantity of rat poison that he had received was the stipulated amount for a unit of battalion strength. With admirable restraint he signalled back to the idiot in Singapore who had made this statement: 'Personnel to strength. Rats in excess of nominal roll.'

Tours were normally of between three and five months; and between December 1962 and August 1966 the Marines of 40 and 42 Cdos. recorded a number of victories in fire-fights, ambushes and defensive actions. It is an 'open secret' that cross-border operations were also conducted.

Throughout the nights of 17 and 21–23 August 1963 Indonesian raiders led by regular troops attacked the *kampong* of Gumbang, only 200 yards inside the border. Defended by a rifle section from L Coy., 42 Cdo. under Sgt. Alastair Mackie, and a section of locally-recruited Border Scouts, the position beat off every attack; and on the night of the 23rd the garrison sortied to place an ambush which caught 60 raiders on their way to the village.

In February 1964, L Coy. of 42 Cdo. and B Coy. of 1/2nd Gurkha Rifles played a part in Operation 'Dragon's Teeth' which was launched against between 30 and 40 Indonesians who had crossed into the Lundu district of Borneo. In a deadly game of hide-and-seek they killed five of the enemy, wounded seven, and captured four, including the regular army NCO who was leading the platoon. The rest of the group was thought to have recrossed the border, but it was suspected that they might have moved into the Sempadi Forest Reserve between Lundu and Kuching. Within a few days their presence was confirmed by the sighting of strange lights to the north of L Coy.'s position at Rasau. The hunt which followed developed into a 'paper-chase' along a trail of discarded enemy ration packs and sweet wrappers. A mixed force of Marines and Gurkhas under Lts. Ashdown and Kakraprasad located an enemy camp on 6 March. As the assault was being prepared, an Indonesian emerged from the camp to fill his water-bottle, and was shot. A fierce fire-fight developed, and the enemy withdrew leaving a casualty and a ton of equipment, weapons and ammunition. More

Wounded Marines from the Limbang action await unloading from the lighter. (Capt. D. A. Oakley)

These men have just come out of the jungle—and it shows . . . The Reconnaissance Troop of 40 Cdo. RM after a patrol on the Indonesian border in 1966. Note the Armalite rifles; and the 'belt order' made up from aircraft quick-release straps recovered from parachute drops.

enemy were believed to have been hit, and for several days the local Dyak tribesmen reported finding bodies in or near the river, some with gunshot wounds.

The tracker dogs, first used in Cyprus, proved invaluable in jungle operations. A team consisted of a team leader (an officer or sergeant), two Iban guides, a tracker dog and handler, an infantry patrol dog and handler, a signaller and four 'cover' men. A team under Sgt. Howe of 42 Cdo. located an Indonesian camp on 21 March 1964, but their dog failed to point in time, and the team were caught in a fire-fight with some 40 enemy troops including light mortar crews. Shooting lasted until dusk, when the Marines withdrew; there were subsequent reports of enemy wounded crossing back into Indonesian territory.

Typically of this kind of jungle 'hide-and-seek', long periods of exertion and surveillance would be followed by brief, savage encounters at short range. This kind of fighting placed a heavy burden on troop commanders and section leaders. On 31 December 1963 a four-man patrol from 40 Cdo. encountered a large group of the enemy—either terrorists under Indonesian leadership, or regular Indonesian troops—and lost one man dead in the course of a fight which ended with the enemy being forced back over the border. In March 1966, almost at the end of the campaign, 42 Cdo. had an officer and a Marine seriously wounded and a second officer killed in a violent action. [The fatality was Lt. Ian Clark, a personal friend of the editor of this series; a fine officer, he left a bride of less than a year expecting the child he never saw.]

East African Interlude

While 40 and 42 Cdo. were serving in the Far East, and 45 Cdo. in the Middle East, a number of army mutinies occurred in East African states which, as former British colonies, retained treaty links with the United Kingdom. As the UK Spearhead Battalion, on call for emergency deployment, 41 Cdo. was recalled from a pay night leave on 4 January 1964 to be emplaned and flown to Kenya within 48 hours. The mutiny did not materialise, and three weeks later 41 Cdo. moved to Tanganyika.

The Marines of 45 Cdo. had more to do at Colito Barracks in Dar-es-Salaam when they landed on 25

Royal Marines in jungle 'bashas' along a ridge path in Borneo. The close country, and short ranges at which 'fire-fights' took place during the so-called Confrontation, can be judged by the thickness of the bamboo and secondary growth here. In primary jungle the going could be much easier, however.

105mm Pack Howitzer of 29 Cdo.Regt. RA—possibly 145 (Maiwand) Bty.—in action in Borneo. The original caption reads 'One into Indonesia'. For political and diplomatic reasons it was always claimed at the time of the Confrontation that British and Commonwealth operations were strictly limited to the Malaysian side of the border—an unmarked border, in thickly jungled mountains . . . In fact, the so-called 'Claret' operations took the war vigorously to the enemy.

Royal Marines prepare to move off on patrol: Borneo, 1964. The man on the left has an A41 radio strapped to a packframe. Webbing is of the light '44 pattern favoured for jungle operations.

January. Mutineers there were awoken by the small arms fire of Z Coy. directed into a safe area, air-burst shellfire from HMS *Cambrian*, and thunder-flashes. The only direct exchange was a 3.5in. anti-tank rocket fired into the guard room to suppress the mutineers' small arms fire. X Coy. took control of the airfield, while Y Coy. and the Cdo. HQ went into the town. Helicopters from HMS *Centaur* lifted troops to other parts of the island to round up mutineers. 41 Cdo. relieved 45; and when they withdrew on 6 April, President Julius Nyere paid the Commandos a generous tribute for their prompt and humane action.

Evolution and Innovation

While the Royal Marines were exercising their special skills around the world in the 1950s to 1970s, the Corps was naturally undergoing a steady series of changes.

In overall strength, the Corps shrank from 11,000 in 1953, to 8,500 during the 1960s, and to 7,000 (with a further 1,000 in the RM Reserve) in 1974. 43 Cdo. was disbanded in 1968; and 41 Cdo. in 1981. The Commando Carrier concept has already been described. HMS *Bulwark*, commissioned in 1960, was joined in 1961 by HMS *Albion*, which served until 1973. In that year HMS *Hermes* (24,000

tons) completed her conversion to the Commando rôle; in 1976/77 she was again converted, this time to a hybrid Commando/anti-submarine capability to take advantage of her helicopter complement. HMS *Bulwark* went into reserve in 1976, being recommissioned between 1979 and 1981. HMS *Hermes* was converted for V/STOL jets in 1980/81.

The introduction of the Landing Platform Docks (LPDs) HMS *Fearless* and *Intrepid* (11,000 tons) in the late 1960s was a logical step from the Commando Carrier principle. These vessels, based on the American LSD, were initially seen as more suited to the Army, since they have the capability of landing armoured vehicles and trucks. As the Falklands campaign was to demonstrate, however, the techniques of amphibious operations are enshrined in Royal Marine training, and the expertise of 3 Cdo.Bde. made the best use of the two LPDs. Each ship is capable of landing a battalion-sized unit and their equipment. They can handle two or three helicopters each; and eight landing craft, four LCVPs being carried on davits and four LCUs 'swimming' out from an internal stern dock in the hull. The LPD can also be used as a floating offshore HQ, as it has accommodation and communications equipment for the brigade head-quarters.

Commando weapons were also changing, along-side those of the Army. The Self-Loading Rifle came into service in the late 1950s—though the men of 40 Cdo. recalled ruefully that they had to exchange the FN semi-automatic rifles which they were 'trialling' for the old bolt-action Lee-Enfield

During the Confrontation, a mixed force of Royal Marines and Gurkha Rifles prepare to embark in Wessex helicopters of the Fleet Air Arm. Navy pilots were popular with all arms for their willingness to fly in marginal conditions to extract men from the jungle after arduous patrolling.

No.4 when preparing for the Suez operation. The Vickers MMG departed, mourned by veteran machinegunners, to be replaced by the lighter and more versatile GPMG. However, the Commandos did hang on to their Bren LMGs; this venerable weapon's box magazine makes it less prone to malfunctions caused by ice or dirt than the 7.62mm link of the GPMG, and it is thus ideal for Arctic and jungle operations. Re-barrelled to take 7.62mm ammunition, the LMG now uses a straight 30-round box or, in emergencies, the 20-round magazine of the rifleman's SLR. The 3.5in. rocket launcher was replaced by the Carl Gustav 84mm anti-tank weapon; and the 3in. mortar by the more accurate and versatile 81mm weapon. It was not until the 1980s, however, that the Commandos received the Milan anti-tank missile system to replace their Wombat anti-tank guns.

Ulster since 1969

The current round of sectarian troubles in Northern Ireland date from the summer of 1969; and in September of that year 41 Cdo., as Spearhead Battalion of the Strategic Reserve, moved from Plymouth to Belfast. This was the first of many emergency tours, but not the first time that Royal Marines had served in Ulster. During the 1956–62 IRA campaign a team visited naval establishments to advise on defence of key points. In December 1956 a composite troop from the NCOs' school was based on HMS *Sea Eagle* in Londonderry; they were relieved by a troop from 42 Cdo. in 1957, and troops subsequently rotated through *Sea Eagle*.

The emergency deployment to Northern Ireland was to become a regular part of the training and operations calendar of all the Commandos from 1969 onwards. 41 Cdo. were in the province for only six weeks in 1969, but a year later 45 Cdo. arrived in Belfast for their first four-month tour. Subsequent four-month tours followed for 40, 41, 42 and 45 Commandos. Sometimes the Marines were faced by rioting sectarian groups: here the baton, shield, CS grenade and baton-gun were the tools of the trade. Patrolling by night and by day also allowed them to gather information and to assert their presence during more troubled periods. A corporal from 40 Cdo. recalls: 'Humour plays a big part in Northern Ireland. Tight discipline, good humour and a laugh sometimes have more effect than 10 rubber bullets.'

This section commander also recalls the problem of searches: 'It takes about three hours to search the average house thoroughly, and that means a long, boring wait for the Marines forming the cordon. It also allows time for a gunman to get into position and shoot at a Marine who is getting tired and losing his concentration.'

Duty in observation posts is another static but absolutely necessary task. Both overt sand-bagged 'sangars' and covert OPs in derelict houses provide valuable information about the habits and contacts of suspects. This patient accumulation of detail can build up into an impressively thorough picture in the operations room of a unit which knows its area and has had plenty of time to 'get picturised'.

Patrolling by day involves tactical movement, with one part of the four-man 'brick' stationary in a good fire position while the other moves along a street or across waste ground. At night, 'We found that the opposition disliked intensely our soft-shoe patrols . . . As long as they knew where we were and how many we were, then they were happy. Four Marines in loose order creeping around the streets threw them into confusion.'

Both 40 and 42 Cdos. were involved in Operation 'Motorman' on 31 July 1972—at the time, the largest operation undertaken by the Army and Royal Marines since Suez. 'Motorman' was intended to re-assert the British Government's authority in both the Republican and the Loyalist 'No-Go' areas of Belfast and Londonderry. The mission for battalion and Commando COs was to 'establish a continuing presence in all hard areas in order to dominate extremists and thus neutralise their ability to influence events until a political settlement had been achieved.'

Some 24 hours before H-Hour a cordon surrounding Londonderry was established by the Ulster Defence Regt. and mobile patrols. This was tightened progressively until, at H−2 hours, several areas had been completely sealed off. In Belfast 42 Cdo. had been tasked with the Ligoniel district, and 40 Cdo. the New Lodge area. With the assistance of bulldozers, and in some cases that of the local population, the barricades were demolished. The security forces suffered no casualties during 'Motorman', although two terrorists were shot dead; 32 weapons were recovered, along with more than 1,000 rounds of ammunition, 450lbs of explosive and 27 bombs.

By the end of 1980 the Royal Marines had made 22 emergency tours in Ulster; 11 officers and men had been killed and more than 80 wounded. A George Medal for gallantry was among the many decorations awarded to men of the Corps.

Tours in Northern Ireland remain an irritant, as Marines have to familiarise themselves with changing 'standard operational procedures' as the political situation alters. Taken together with

41 Cdo., 'T' Block, Turf Lodge Estate, West Belfast, 1978. Left to right: L/Cpl. Bold, 'brick' commander; Lt.Col. T. Secombe, OBE, commanding 41 Cdo. RM; and Capt. B. J. Hawgood, commanding F Coy., 41 Cdo. The Pye Pocketfone, Northern Ireland boots, and collared flak jackets with non-slip rifle butt pads are all innovations since the 1969 photograph. (Capt. B. J. Hawgood)

A mobile patrol of 45 Cdo. RM in Turf Lodge in 1977. The air-portable $\frac{1}{4}$ ton Land Rover is stripped of doors and tailgate to allow instant deployment. The Marine watching the rear has a SUIT (Sighting Unit Trilux) mounted on his SLR. Since it lacks a lead or harness, the dog would appear to be a social acquaintance taken along for the ride!

Marines of 41 Cdo. RM talk to local children in Belfast, 1969. Their respirator and flak jacket patterns indicate the vintage of this very early Ulster scene. So do the early 'jerseys, heavyweight', which had a draw-string at the neck, and reinforcement at the cuffs as well as the shoulders and elbows.

training abroad, Ulster service can also mean long periods of separation from home bases and next-of-kin: on occasion Marines have deployed from Mountain and Arctic training in Norway, to Northern Ireland training, and then straight to the province for a four-month tour.

IRA terrorists attempted to score a propaganda coup on 17 October 1981 by placing a booby-trap bomb in the car of the Commandant General Royal Marines, Lt.Gen. Sir Steuart Pringle, outside his home. The bomb exploded; but although the CGRM suffered grave leg injuries, he hung on to life by sheer strength of character as he was cut out of the wreck. His return to his duties until his retirement in 1984 remains an inspiration to all those who have been maimed by terrorist acts or on active service.

Training and Exercises

Prior to 1970 RM recruits underwent initial training at the Deal depot before proceeding to the Commando Training Centre at Lympstone; but now all recruits—including Junior Marines aged between 16 and $17\frac{1}{2}$—join at Lympstone.

Recruits are trained to look after themselves and their equipment, so that they can operate in isolation from their parent Commando; thus, small Ships Detachments or Naval Parties retain their own identity and efficiency. (This high level of self-reliance once caused a mother to complain of feelings of inadequacy and redundance when her son returned home on his first leave from Commando training. After washing and ironing his clothing and tidying his room, he offered to lend a hand in 'the galley' . . .)

There is, of course, a strong emphasis on physical fitness in the Corps. The sight of a Marine on an afternoon run after work, accompanied by his dog, is very common around RM barracks: 'There are a lot of very fit dogs around here', as one commented.

More specialist training includes an RM sniper course lasting five weeks. It is largely due to the Corps that the special skills of the military sniper, apart from the basic requirement of outstanding marksmanship, did not disappear from the British forces during the early post-war decades. The Army had to come to the Marines for help when experience in Northern Ireland made clear the Army's need to re-establish sniper training. Other specialist training carried out at Lympstone includes instruction in NBC techniques; the related hazards peculiar to NBC warfare in Arctic conditions are also covered, and developed when on exercise in Norway.

Mountain and Arctic Warfare

The public have seen the Corps demonstrate cliff assault techniques at the Royal Tournament over many years since the 1950s, and this is the 'popular face' of a very demanding skill retained and developed in the Corps since the Second World War by the specialists of the Commando Cliff Assault Wing RM. Active duty in the Middle East and Far East in the 1950s and 1960s emphasised the value of climbing skills and abseiling from helicopters. The concept of the Reconnaissance Leader (RL) was developed within the Wing during the 1960s, and taught to the men of the Commando Recce Troops. It involved cliff assault, winter survival, sniping and reconnaissance techniques, and close contact with Norwegian forces enabled the Wing to learn more about the skills peculiar to fighting in extreme cold.

In 1971 the Wing was redesignated Mountain and Arctic Warfare Cadre; in the interim it has moved from its original barracks at Stonehouse, Plymouth, to Lympstone, thence to 45 Cdo.Gp. at Arbroath, and in 1982 back to Stonehouse. In the late 1960s, as 3 Cdo.Bde. became earmarked to the Northern Flank of NATO, the M&AW Cadre faced the daunting task of passing on their special skills to the Commandos. The first to be M&AW trained was 45 Cdo.Gp. in 1969; 42 Cdo. followed in 1977, and the remainder of the brigade in 1978. The Cadre provided instructors to company and unit level, and advised on training programmes.

In Operation 'Corporate' in the South Atlantic in 1982 the Cadre was a 3 Cdo.Bde. HQ intelligence and recce asset; and the brigade's intelligence cell remembers its information as just as valuable and reliable than that provided by the SAS and SBS. Under the command of Capt. Rod Boswell the Cadre had a small but famous fire-fight with a group of Argentine Marine Commando special forces at the farm of Top Malo House.

Arctic and Tropics

It is in Norway that a vital part of the training of 3 Cdo. Bde. units takes place each year. The first deployment to NATO's Northern Flank took place in January 1970, when an advance party of 45 Cdo.

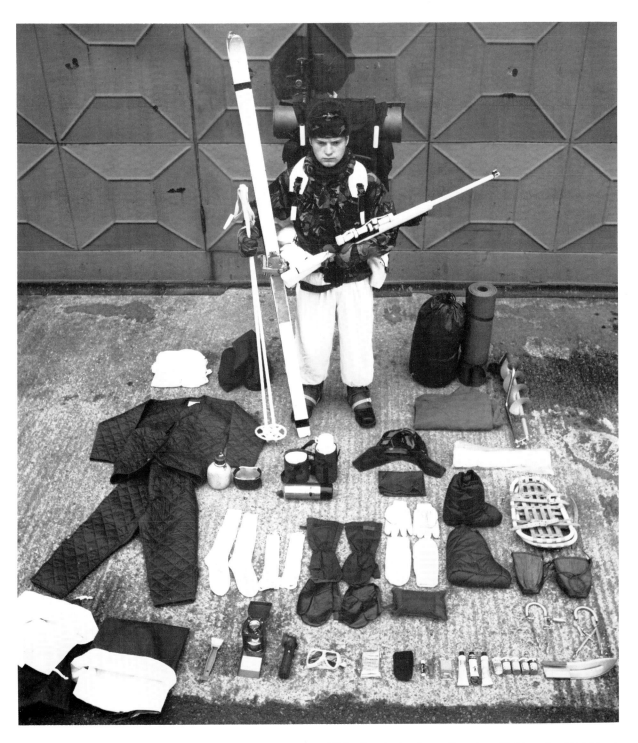

arrived at Elvergardsmoen Camp near Narvik in northern Norway. Since then the Corps has returned each year for three months' training. The Corps aims to take men without M&AW training to Norway, so that there is a period at the beginning of the deployment when experience and skills are learned 'on the ground' in time for a final, full

RM sniper in Arctic warfare rig, with his entire kit laid out. The total cost of this equipment is in the region of £500, apart from any private purchases the men may make. Visible here are items including a vacuum flask and cover, ski wax, sleeping mat and Arctic sleeping bag, and windproof, waterproof, insulated and camouflage clothing. Webbing, and L42A1 rifle, are camouflaged with white tape. (Pete Holdgate)

NATO exercise in the north each March.

Instruction is by Military Ski Instructors and

Royal Marine of 45 Cdo. on a ski march. He wears the full 'whites', including a cover over the rucksack. The lightweight white nylon snow camouflage clothing is popular, as it allows snow to be brushed off easily. The double-sling arrangement allows the SLR to be slung over the pack. (Martin May, 45 Cdo.)

Mountain Leaders. The Marines learn the secrets of ski-wax, and the techniques of cross-country skiing with a weapon and back pack. Living in the snow follows a 'decreasing curve' of comfort from the comparative luxury of a ten-man tent, through the tent sheet, to the snow hole: it is an environment in which the phrase 'fight to survive, and survive to fight' has a very real meaning. It is essential that men work in pairs, so that they can watch each other for signs of frostbite. As the author was told: 'It is not a crime to be cold in the Arctic—but not to tell anyone, is.'

The whole of 3 Cdo.Bde., except for 40 Cdo., can deploy to Norway at any time during the year. The Commandos are supported by the Cdo. Logistic Regt. RM, 3 Cdo.Bde. Air Sqn. RM, 29 Cdo.Regt. RA, and 59 Independent Cdo.Sqn. RE.

Since 1970 the Royal Marines have deployed on exercise around the world. In that year they participated in 'Bersatu Padu'—the last large-scale jungle exercise to be held by British forces. (It was in the Malayan jungle that an alert but nervous Marine on watch in the half-light roused the troop when he saw figures moving towards their position. The enemy intruders were revealed as two ambling orang-outangs.)

Jungle skills are retained within the Corps by the annual 'Curry Trail' exercise held in Brunei. A composite company is sent, with its own instructors, on a course which ends with a jungle exercise with the Gurkhas. Marines with experience of the two extremes of Norway and Brunei say that they prefer the cold of the former: at least in the Arctic a man can get warm, while in the sauna-bath atmosphere of the jungle there is almost no way to get cooler.

Exercises have also taken the Corps to Sardinia, Greece, Turkey, Canada, and Holland—and here the Marines have a chance to re-affirm their long-standing friendship with the Royal Netherlands Marines, or 'Cloggies'. The RNLMC's 'Whisky' Coy. serves under command as part of 45 Cdo., for NATO operations, in a unique example of inter-allied co-operation. Individuals from the RNLMC are regularly attached to the Royal Marines as troop sergeants, or attend RM courses; and the 1st Amphibious Combat Group RNLMC—equivalent to a Commando—has an integral rôle under 3 Cdo.Bde. HQ for NATO operations.

Another connection of long standing which is regularly renewed—among other occasions, by the

105mm Light Gun of 29 Cdo.Regt. RA mounted on skis, and towed by a BV202 oversnow vehicle. The gun's ability to fire airburst shells is invaluable in conditions where point-fuzed shells lose most of their effect in the snow. The Light Gun can also be heli-lifted to firing positions. (Pete Holdgate)

1: RM Commando, Cyprus, mid-1950s
2: RM Commando, 45 Cdo.RM; Port Said, 1956
3: Cpl.,RM Commandos, UK, mid-1950s

1

2

3

A

1: Cpl., RM Commandos, Borneo,
early 1960s
2: L/Cpl., RM Cdo. Ship Detachment;
Far East, early 1960s
3: RM Commando, Brunei, 1984

1

2

3

B

1: RM Commando, 41 Cdo. RM;
   UN duty, Cyprus, 1974
2: GPMG number, 45 Cdo. RM;
   Radfan Mts., 1964
3: Lt.Col.RM, HMS Britannia, 1970s

1

2

3

C

2: RM recruit, 1980s

3: MA Wren, 1980s

1: Cpl., RM Commandos,
41 Cdo. RM; UK, 1980

4: Sgt., RM Commandos, 1980s

5: Lt., RM Commandos;
mess dress, UK, 1980s

D

1: RSM, RM Commandos, UK, 1980s
2: Drum-major, RM School of Music, 1980s
3: 2nd Lt., 40 Cdo. RM; UK, 1980s

1

2

3

E

1: Lt., 42 Cdo. RM; Norway, 1984
2: LMG number, RM Commandos; East Falkland, 1982

1: Rigid Raider coxswain, Falklands, 1982
2: Helicopter pilot, 3 Cdo. Bde. Air Sqn.;
   Falklands, 1982
3: Sapper, 59 Indep. Cdo. Sqn. RE; Falklands, 1982

G

1: RM Commando sniper, 1980s
2: RM Commando rifleman, 198?
3: RM Commando 84 mm A/T crew, 1980s
4: RM Commando, N. Ireland, 1980s

H

joint Rum Punch exercises which have been held in Puerto Rico since 1971—is with the United States Marine Corps. The two Corps served together in Korea in 1950–52, and have a similar commitment to the NATO Northern Flank. (A healthy attitude of friendly rivalry is indicated by the fact that when occasionally asked by their US counterparts what the 'R' in 'RM' stands for, Commandos tend to reply: '*Real* Marines'.)

In 1974 and 1979, 41 Cdo. went to Cyprus on United Nations duty. Wearing the blue beret of the UN Peace-Keeping forces, they served two six-month tours along the border between Greek and Turkish areas—work which required the skills of the diplomat and the policeman.

In July 1974 40 Cdo. also went to Cyprus, but wearing a different hat: that of Britain's 'Spearhead Battalion', which is on call for rapid deployment anywhere in the world. In this rôle, which lasts for a month at a time, each Commando has a rifle company and CO's tactical headquarters ready to fly to any trouble-spot within 24 hours; the other two rifle companies, support company and attached artillery battery and administration elements follow within 72 hours. In Cyprus in 1974 40 Cdo. was tasked with reinforcing the British Western Sovereign Base at Akrotiri at the time of the Turkish landings in the north of the island. They guarded the perimeter, and did valuable work regulating vehicle traffic and refugees at a time of tension and unrest.

Combat and Logistic Support

Not everyone who wears a green beret pins a globe-and-laurel badge on it. The gunners of 29 Cdo.Regt. RA, the sappers of 59 Indep.Cdo.Sqn. RE, and the many different specialists of the Cdo. Logistic Regt. RM are all vital parts of 3 Cdo.Bde., supporting the Commandos in the field and keeping their beachheads operating.

Though 29 Field Regt. RA had been in existence since the early 1950s, it was not until 1961 that the Royal Marines asked the Royal Artillery if they could provide support for the Corps. The regiment was regrouped from around the world, and in 1962 the gunners were Commando-trained; in May of

An 81mm mortar of the Heavy Weapons Troop of 45 Cdo. RM, live-firing in Norway, 1984. Arctic conditions impose special requirements on the mortar crew: the base plate has to be bedded into snow that is well packed, but not frozen so hard that it cannot absorb the recoil of the tube. The Marines are wearing 'moon boots'—flat-soled insulated boots, worn over the Ski-March boots. (Pete Holdgate)

that year they received their green berets from the CGRM at a parade held to welcome **29 Cdo.Regt. RA** to the Corps. By the end of the year the regiment was in action in the Far East, and was the first unit of the RA to fire the 105mm Pack Howitzer in anger. Between 1962 and 1972 batteries served in Malaya, Singapore, Brunei, Sarawak and Hong Kong; and elements were also embarked aboard HMS *Bulwark*, *Albion*, *Intrepid* and *Fearless*. In its Commando Carrier rôle the unit developed helicopter mobility, with under-slung guns and ammunition, allowing the lifting of howitzers to remote areas inaccessible by road, and the rapid build-up of a beachhead defence.

Parts of 29 Cdo.Regt. supported 2 Para in Bahrain and Aden in 1965–66; and, like other units of the Royal Artillery, its personnel have served emergency tours in the infantry rôle in Northern Ireland since 1971. During the Falklands campaign the complete regiment gave invaluable support to the men of 3 Cdo.Bde. and 5 Inf.Bde., with the still comparatively new 105mm Light Gun.

Some batteries are co-located with the Commandos that they support: the Arctic-trained 7 (Sphinx) Cdo.Bty. are at Arbroath with 45 Cdo. 8 (Alma) Cdo.Bty. returned from Malta in 1977 and are now at the Royal Citadel, Plymouth. Also at the Royal Citadel is 79 (Kirkee) Cdo.Bty., who have an Arctic rôle with 42 Cdo.

A specialised, and (until the Falklands) often forgotten part of the regiment is 148 (Meiktila)

A Rigid Raider at speed in a Norwegian fjord. These small but powerful boats allow men and stores to be landed on small beaches, and can be driven up the beach beyond high-water mark by their own velocity. (Martin May, 45 Cdo.)

Cdo. Forward Observation Bty., based at Poole. They have no guns of their own, but operate ashore, calling down naval gunfire support on land targets; NGS was of vital importance in the capture of South Georgia, the raid on Pebble Island and the final battles for the high ground around Stanley. The men of 148 Bty. are trained parachutists and divers, and can also work as controllers for fighter/ground-attack aircraft. Ten naval ratings form an integral part of the battery.

The Commando Artillery Regiment also has under command 289 Cdo.Bty. (Volunteers) in East Ham, London—the only Territorial Army battery under direct command of a regular regiment.

Based at Plymouth, with a field troop detached to 45 Cdo. at Arbroath, is **59 Independent Commando Squadron, Royal Engineers**. From 1968 to 1971 59 Field Sqn. RE, as it then was, gave engineer support to 3 Cdo.Bde. RM; with the beginning of the withdrawal from 'East of Suez' in 1971 the unit was re-formed at Plymouth as 59 Indep.Cdo.Sqn., and made part of the brigade order of battle. Squadron personnel are selected for maturity and experience from among Royal Engineer volunteers; they are then required to pass the All Arms Commando course which entitles them to wear the green beret. When they return to their parent units soldiers, sappers and gunners retain the Army's red-dagger-on-blue Commando sleeve badge.

Though the Commandos have their own Assault Engineers—organic units equivalent to the Assault Pioneers within an Army infantry battalion—59 Cdo.Sqn. have the training and equipment for the major engineering tasks within the brigade area. This work includes mine-laying and clearance, booby-traps, route maintenance and denial, bridging and rafting, water supply, and snow clearance. Bulk fuel storage in a Beach Support Area is another RE responsibility, so the squadron has a full diving team for the reconnaissance of beaches. During the Falklands campaign, experience demonstrated that there was a need for the Engineers to be able to work with the Recce troops of their Commandos to locate and identify minefields and mine types. With its own REME workshops, the squadron's strength is nine officers and 253 soldiers. Territorial forces include 131 Indep. Cdo. Sqn. RE(V).

The **Commando Logistic Regiment** was set up between July 1971 and January 1972, to provide

A Marine in Brunei during Operation 'Curry Trail'. He wears a jungle hat, which has taken on its own character, and DPM jungle and tropical issue uniform soaked to a black-green by sweat. (Author's photo)

a wide range of support for the brigade in their UK base, or on operations up to brigade size. It includes officers and men of seven different corps, with about 70 per cent of Royal Marines, and all personnel are Commando-trained. The regiment has five squadrons: Headquarters, Medical, Transport, Ordnance and Workshop.

The HQ Sqn. is based in the Brigade Maintenance Area in wartime, and is tasked with controlling the BMA and executing the logistic plan of the Bde. HQ. In the Falklands the loss of *Atlantic Conveyor*, and with her a major part of the helicopter lift capability, gave the 'Loggies' a serious problem: resources were limited, roads were non-existent, and the ground was very 'poor going'.

The Medical Sqn., with its Royal Navy Surgical Support Teams, became famous in the Falklands as the 'Red and Green Life Machine'—the 'Red' being a reference to the Para doctors who worked alongside Cdr. 'Rick' Jolly's green-beret personnel. The squadron gives first-line medical support to the BMA and B Echelon, and second-line support to the Regimental Aid Posts as their casualties are cleared. If there are delays they give support and stabilisation before evacuation.

The Transport Sqn. give second-line support to the Commandos and attached elements, and move combat supplies and other support stores and equipment from the BSA and BMA to Distribution Points or to units. They also occasionally provide troop-carrying vehicles.

The Ordnance Sqn. has two months'-worth of MT & Tech. Stores 'on wheels'. Combat Supply Troops run the stock control at the BMA and Distribution Points. Bulk distribution of fresh and composition rations, ammunition and POL is an Ordnance Sqn. responsibility, as is the provision of Local Resources Teams to buy stores locally.

The Workshop Sqn. repair vehicles, electronic equipment and instruments, carry out light recovery, and service the BV202 oversnow vehicle. (They brought back from the Falklands a compact diesel tractor of Italian design, captured broken down and unusable, which now earns its keep pushing and pulling 'dead' vehicles.) The squadron's Arctic work has special hazards—in sub-zero temperatures there is a constant danger of bare skin freezing on to metal, while towing vehicles can cause further damage in these conditions: so the

Cpl. Sullivan and Lt. Milne photographed during 'Curry Trail': as jungle-trained Marines they are part of the Directing Staff on navigation exercises. Cpl. Sullivan, photographed at his ease, wears temperate climate boots with jungle-issue uniform. Lt. Milne, wearing the older-issue cellular shirt, is pouring oil from a ration can of fish onto the bamboo fire which keeps mosquitoes at bay. (Author's photo)

Oversnow Troop take their tools to the job, rather than having the BV202s brought to them.

During the Falklands campaign the Cdo. Logistic Regt. moved 9,000 tons of stores in the Ajax Bay BMA, which was 400m square. Also under its control in the area were 12 attached units and sub-units including a Rapier SAM battery, a PoW cage, an Engineer Support Section and Water Point, and a Satellite Communications Detachment. The regiment suffered one dead and 26 wounded during an air attack on 27 May 1982; it received two OBEs and four Mentions in Despatches.

The **3 Cdo. Bde. Air Sqn. RM**—or 'BAS' (Brigade Air Squadron)—was formed on 12 August 1968 at Sembawang, Singapore; at that time it was equipped with Sioux Mk.1 helicopters, being an amalgamation of the then Bde. Flight, 40 Cdo. RM Air Troop, 42 Cdo. RM Air Troop and 29 Cdo.Lt.Regt. RA Air Observation Post Troop. In 1970 the squadron also received four Scout AH Mk.1, and in the UK the 41 Cdo. and 45 Cdo. Air Troops were amalgamated with it, to give 18 aircraft in a mix of anti-tank and reconnaissance types. In 1974–75 the Sioux was replaced by 12 Gazelle AH Mk.1; anti-tank capability was provided by SS11 missiles. By 1982 there were plans

Two faces of exhaustion: Brunei, 1983. The older Marine, a member of the Brigade Air Defence Troop, rests at a checkpoint suffering from dehydration and exhaustion—he later pushed on to rejoin his patrol. The younger man has just climbed up to a ridge line under the full strength of a tropical midday sun. (Author's photos)

to replace the SS11-armed Scout with six TOW-armed Lynx. The Falklands intervened, and the squadron was posted south, where it gave valuable service. Two Gazelles were shot down, and three men killed, during the San Carlos landings; and thereafter the rôle of light helicopters was re-evaluated. The venerable Scouts saw front-line action in the last hours of fighting, attacking an Argentine artillery position with SS11 ASMs.

The BAS is the largest light helicopter squadron in the British armed forces. Flights formerly bore the names of battle honours associated with the unit they supported: 'Brunei' (29 Cdo. Regt. RA), 'Dieppe' (40 Cdo. RM), 'Salerno' (41 Cdo. RM), 'Kangaw' (42 Cdo. RM) and 'Montforterbeek' (45 Cdo. RM). Since 1981/82 flights are identified simply by letters: currently A and C Flts. each have six Gazelles and B Flt. has an establishment of six Lynxs. The squadron has very close links with the Fleet Air Arm and the Army Air Corps, and among its personnel may be seen the badges of the REME, RAOC, RA, RN and WRNS, among others. Flying skills are of a high order, demanded by the squadron's required ability to operate off ships' flight decks, out of jungle clearings resembling 'green lift shafts', in the Arctic conditions of the Norwegian winter, and in the mist and rain of Northern Ireland (where the BAS has sent flights on 18 operational tours to date).

The **Raiding Squadron RM** were originally part of the Landing Craft Branch of the Royal Marines, but in 1972 they came under command of the HQ & Signals Sqn. of 3 Cdo.Bde. RM. There

were at that time two squadrons, but in the late 1970s one was disbanded, to be re-formed as a squadron within the Royal Marine Reserve. No.3 Raiding Sqn. was also formed for work in Hong Kong.

Early work had been in inflatable rubber craft—the Gemini, with Johnson 30hp OBM—which could be stowed aboard submarines, and inflated on the casing for launching. The fibreglass Rigid Raider, with a more powerful outboard, has since largely replaced the IRC. Operating in Norwegian waters poses exposure injury risks for the coxswains, who need an immersion suit and other protective clothing. During the Falklands campaign the Raiding Sqn., under Capt. Chris Baxter, did valuable service inserting personnel of various 'advance parties', and, less dramatically, in San Carlos Water running a 'taxi' service between ships at anchor. At the close of the campaign they landed men of Boat Troop, D Sqn., 22 SAS and an SBS team on the eastern end of Wireless Ridge in a violent diversionary raid in support of 2 Para's attack on the western end of the feature.

Also under command of the HQ & Signals Sqn. is the **Air Defence Tp.** armed with Blowpipe surface-to-air missiles. Criticism of this weapon in the aftermath of the campaign does not detract from the courage and stamina of the men who carried it. At Goose Green an eyewitness recalled the Royal Marines standing up under fire in order to get a better shot at a Pucara as it began a strafing run against 2 Para; they brought it down—perhaps a partial revenge for the shooting down of one of the BAS's Scouts by a Pucara earlier in the action.

Assault Squadrons
The Royal Marines have manned landing craft since 1943, and these skills have been retained in the Corps' work with the LPDs HMS *Fearless* and *Intrepid*. The Assault Sqn. aboard *Intrepid* ferried relief stores during operations to assist victims of flooding on the Ganges; in more warlike circumstances they were to use their skills to bring men and stores ashore during Operation 'Corporate'.

Assault Beach Units in Assault Sqns. carry vehicles to lay Class 40 trackway, a flexible metal sheet which allows vehicles to drive over soft ground. BARVs—a class of vehicle pioneered on D-Day in June 1944—are now based on a Centurion tank chassis, and can winch bogged or flooded vehicles out of the water. The Assault Sqns. have a high proportion of officers and NCOs, since their personnel are required to crew and command LCUs and LCVPs. Tragically, on the same day that the LSLs *Sir Galahad* and *Sir Tristram* were attacked at Fitzroy, Argentine A-4s hit LCU 'F4' and killed four Marines and two naval ratings.

On a lighter note, it may be mentioned that during briefings and training for the San Carlos landings the men of The Parachute Regiment decided that the LCVP, with its ramped bow, was obviously a rubbish skip; and thereafter, to the irritation of the RM coxswains, amphibious operations were dubbed 'rubbish skipping'!

In a re-organisation of 1984 a new squadron was created which included the Raiding Sqn., two LCUs and four LCVPs, under the command of Maj. E. Southby-Tailyour. (Southby-Tailyour is the spare-time yachtsman whose charting of the Falklands' intricate coastline for his own interest during a previous tour as commander of NP 8901 proved to be of such value to 3 Cdo.Bde. HQ during the preparation of Operation 'Sutton'.) Designated 539 Assault Sqn. RM, it will be a 3 Cdo.Bde. asset capable of lifting men and equipment during training and operations on the Northern Flank.

* * *

Comacchio Group

Helicopter and amphibious skills of a very high order are required for one of the Royal Marines' more unusual tasks: protecting the rigs of Britain's offshore oil resources in the North Sea. On 20 July 1977, L Coy., 42 Cdo. deployed in the 'Oilsafe' Programme; and in May 1980 Comacchio Coy. RM was formed with the task of protecting the rigs and other installations. Now redesignated Comacchio Group, the unit has seven rifle troops each of 32 all ranks. Training includes landing on oil platforms by sea and air, and then clearing the structure through its stores, pump rooms, offices and work areas. The Marines work in smoke and CS gas environments, with booby-traps and live firing drills, while keeping in constant contact by radio.

Comacchio Gp., and all Royal Marine Commandos, have a close affinity with Naval Air

An 81mm mortar during live firing practice on Ascension Island prior to the move south to the Falklands, 1982. On Ascension the Marines zeroed their weapons, and put in some tough marching, back-packing weapons such as the 81mm mortar.

Squadrons 845 and 846; originally equipped with the Westland Wessex, they have for several years flown the HC.4 Commando version of the Sea King helicopter.

Ships' Detachments

The rôle of Royal Marines aboard HM warships, of major importance before the Second World War, was retained to some extent after 1945; the last Royal Navy battleship, HMS *Vanguard*, carried as many as 350. However, by 1970 the detachments had been greatly reduced. In 1978 the MoD decided to put small detachments back on to warships, to act as landing parties, fulfil ceremonial duties, and act as guards and buglers during visits to friendly ports. At sea the 'Royals' have sea duty stations and play a full part in the working of the ship, sometimes serving as missile launcher crews. The sergeant commanding the detachment is always known as 'sergeant-major' at sea, and has a corporal and eight Marines under him. In 1981 there were 12 of these detachments at sea. The following year the detachment on the ice protection vessel HMS *Endurance*, with nine men from NP 8901, went into action on South Georgia during the Argentine invasion. *Endurance* carried 13 Marines, a larger detachment than those aboard missile-armed destroyers and frigates.

The Special Boat Squadron

The origins of the SBS lie in the Second World War, when infiltration techniques were pioneered against the German-held coast of France and other European countries. Best known is the attack by RMBPD canoeists on German shipping in Bordeaux in December 1942, later made famous in the book and film *The Cockleshell Heroes*. By July 1944 the Special Boat Section had been formed into A, B and C Groups under the Small Operations Group. The SBS became a Royal Marine unit after the war.

Today the Special Boat Squadron is composed of three sections, one of which is dedicated to anti-terrorist work. Their rôle includes sabotage, reconnaissance and intelligence-gathering. They are trained in diving and parachuting, and still use canoes and small boats. They have a more discreet profile than the SAS, mainly because of their rôle.

In May 1972 a report that bombs had been placed on board the liner *Queen Elizabeth II* led to a team including Royal Marines, presumably of the SBS, being parachuted into the Atlantic to board and check her. During the Falklands campaign the SBS were inserted before the main landings to check beaches for mines and obstacles. They were used to attack the small Argentine garrison at Fanning Head, a headland covering the approaches to San Carlos Water; during this action they used thermal imaging equipment, probably the first occasion that it has been used operationally.

```
┌──────────────────────────────────────────┐
│                                          │
│  Table 3: Reinforced 3 Cdo.Bde., April-May 1982 │
│                                          │
│                    HQ                    │
│                                          │
│  40 Cdo.RM    42 Cdo.RM    45 Cdo.RM     │
│                                          │
│     2 Para              3 Para           │
│                                          │
│  Cdo.Log.Regt.RM      29 Cdo.Regt.RA     │
│                                          │
│  59 Indep.Cdo.Sqn.RE  Bde.HQ&Sigs.Sqn.RM │
│                                          │
│  Band of Cdo.Forces RM   M&AW Cadre RM   │
│                                          │
│  Reinforced Bde.      Medium Recce Tp.,  │
│  Air Sqn.RM           Blues & Royals     │
│                                          │
│  1 Raiding Sqn.RM    T Bty., 12 AD Regt.RA │
│                                          │
│  Royal Signals elements  Surg.Spt.Team RN │
│                                          │
└──────────────────────────────────────────┘
```

The Falklands

All Britain's military endeavours in the South Atlantic started with the Corps: and they started with a battle which might have been an Alamo or a Camerone.

A small detachment of Royal Marines had been stationed on the Falklands since the 1960s, when neighbouring Argentina began to make belligerent noises about the islands. Naval Party 8901, in the person of a 'rotated' garrison of roughly troop strength, guarded the islands and arrested such intruders as arrived by sea or air.

In April 1982 the military *junta* in Buenos Aires implemented a long-standing plan to seize the islands by military force.[1] On the night of 2 April men of the Argentine Special Forces landed by helicopter near the islands' capital, Stanley, on East Falkland and made their way to Moody Brook, the small garrison accommodation of NP 8901. The Royal Marines had vacated their barracks, and the enemy attack with grenades and automatic weapons served only to damage empty buildings.

The Argentines then moved to the Governor's house on the western edge of Stanley. Here they encountered part of NP 8901. Since they included both the incoming 1982–83 garrison as well as the outgoing 1981–82 party, the Royal Marines were at roughly twice their usual strength with 67 men. Elements of this force fought an intense action around Government House.

Meanwhile the bulk of the invasion force had come ashore near the airfield, in approximately brigade strength, supported by American-supplied amphibious APCs. One of the LVTP-7s was knocked out by 84mm and 66mm fire on the road to Stanley. (One of the anti-tank crews recalled that smoke poured out of the vehicle, and 'no one was seen to surface'.)

After several hours' fighting the Governor, Mr Rex Hunt, invoked the 1939 Emergency Powers which named him as commander-in-chief in the event of hostilities; and to avoid the civilian casualties which he feared would be inevitable in a

---

[1] A much fuller account of the whole campaign will be found in MAA 133, *Battle for the Falklands (1): Land Forces*, by the present author. Relevant material will also be found in MAAs 134 and 135, *Naval Forces* and *Air Forces*.

fight to the finish among the houses of Stanley, he ordered the vastly outnumbered Royal Marine garrison to surrender. Though prepared to fight on in Stanley, or to take to the bleak hinterland for continued covert operations, the RM commander, Maj. Michael Norman, reluctantly accepted this order. The photographs of tired, camouflage-smeared Marines being disarmed and searched were deeply felt as an affront in Britain, and contributed to the spirit that sent the Task Force south.

On 3 April Lt. Keith Mills, RM gave the Royal Marines a taste of revenge when his small force of 22 men fought off air and sea attacks on South Georgia. In the course of this action his men downed a Puma helicopter and claimed an Alouette; and achieved a unique distinction when they used their 84mm Carl Gustav anti-tank weapon in an anti-shipping rôle, putting a round close to the waterline of the Argentine frigate *Granville* as it moved into King Edward Cove near Grytviken. Over a thousand small arms rounds also hit the ship, as did a 66mm rocket, which hit the forward gun turret and jammed its training mechanism.

Both the men of NP 8901 and those detached via HMS *Endurance* to South Georgia were later repatriated to the UK via Uruguay.

The Task Force despatched by the British Government within days of the invasion moved south at a steady speed, carrying the men of 40, 42 and 45 Cdos.; their vital artillery and engineer support; and the 'Loggies', whose skills in supporting an amphibious landing and running a beachhead would be central to the success of Operation 'Sutton'—the land phase of the land, sea and air operations designated 'Corporate'.

The men of M Coy., 42 Cdo. travelled aboard Royal Fleet Auxiliaries, their departure kept a discreet secret. With the SAS and SBS, Marines of M Coy. had the distinction of retaking South Georgia on 25/26 April, in an almost bloodless operation which involved inspired bluff, and the courage to seize the opportunity presented by the attack on the Argentine submarine *Santa Fe*. Maj. Guy Sheridan of 42 Cdo. decided to land at once; and with excellent Naval Gunfire Support the SAS and Marines persuaded the Argentine garrison at Grytviken, under their sinister commander Alfredo

San Carlos, early in Operation 'Sutton': a Marine of the Air Defence Troop 'listens out' on his Clansman radio. He wears a civilian waterproof jacket over his Arctic windproof smock and 'TMLs'. Note the hessian camouflage tied round his SLR.

Astiz, to surrender without a fight.

At 1125 hrs on 20 May the men of the Task Force received the signal '*Palpas*'—the codeword for implementing the landing at San Carlos. These landlocked bays had been chosen after long discussion on the journey south: though many miles from the objective of Stanley, they offered protection against air attack and a relatively secure base in which to build up the BMA.

The landing went slower than had been planned, but was unopposed apart from the brief resistance of a small enemy force on Fanning Head. This position at the entrance to San Carlos Water was attacked by the SBS, naval gunfire, and the persuasive Spanish of Capt. Rod Bell, RM. Dressed in immaculate 'pusser's order', Bell stood microphone in hand, appealing to the Argentines to surrender, while the men of the SBS hugged the ground. Of the Argentine soldiers who stayed to fight, all but one were killed or captured. Others of their company caused the first casualty of the landing when they shot down two Gazelle helicopters, killing three of the four men aboard.

As the heavy enemy air attacks developed around the Water and Falkland Sound, the Paras and Royal Marines secured the beachhead. A small but interesting fire-fight took place on 26 May at a farm building called Top Malo House. Nineteen men of the Mountain and Arctic Warfare Cadre attacked this position, which was occupied by 16 men of Argentine Marine Commando Coy. 602. In this clash between the two élite forces, the men of the M&AW Cadre blasted the building with 66mm rockets; the Argentines stormed out, and fought until their two officers became casualties. After the seven wounded and six unwounded survivors surrendered, Capt. Rod Boswell discovered that the surviving enemy officer was not only married to an English girl, but had attended courses in Britain.

The three Commandos ashore on the island had different tasks. 40 Cdo. guarded the BMA at San Carlos—vital, but for the Marines rather frustrating work, involving long but largely uneventful patrols. They thought that with the subsequent arrival of 5 Inf.Bde. they would see fighting around Stanley; but only two companies were detached to the 1st Bn. Welsh Guards after that unit had suffered heavy casualties aboard the *Sir Tristram*.

For the men of 45 Cdo. there was the long, epic 'yomp' across the northern wastes of East Falkland, a march made necessary by the loss of helicopters aboard the *Atlantic Conveyor*. As 45 Cdo. cleared Douglas Settlement and moved along the northern coast, K Coy. of 42 Cdo. were lifted by helicopter in a daring thrust across the island to Mt. Kent, landing in the middle of a fire-fight between the

GPMG crew of 42 Cdo. RM on Mount Harriet. The gunner, Mne. Sean Egan, served with NP 8901 in the defence of Government House in Stanley during the Argentine invasion of early April 1982. His No.2 wears a civilian woollen hat, and a captured Argentine parka.

Argentines and the SAS on 30 May. The arrival of a second company and artillery elements put the Marines within sight of Stanley and with the firepower to engage outlying enemy positions. On 5 June 42 Cdo. started to move on to Mt. Challenger, and 45 Cdo. relieved them on Mt. Kent.

On the night of 11/12 June the men of 3 Cdo. Bde. made a three-pronged attack on enemy positions around Stanley. While 3 Para attacked Mt. Longdon with 2 Para in reserve, 45 Cdo. attacked from Mt. Kent on to Two Sisters, and 42 Cdo. attacked from Mt. Challenger on to Goat Ridge and thence on to Mt. Harriet. Lt.Col. Nick Vaux, commanding 42, decided that he would send his K Coy. along the south of the position to roll up the enemy from east to west—that is, from their rear. L Coy. would exploit the advantage of this attack to overrun forward positions; and finally J Coy., after causing a diversion with MG and Milan fire, would move forward and consolidate.

K Coy. made a silent approach, via a minefield, to the south of Harriet, and were within 100 yards of the enemy before they were detected. The fighting was supported by the guns of HMS *Yarmouth* as well as the 105s of 29 Cdo.Regt. RA. By first light K Coy. had 70 prisoners. L Coy. went uphill through the rocks from south to north, firing Milan anti-tank missiles at bunkers identified by prior reconnaissance. At dawn J Coy. swept through the positions to clear any remaining enemy; within two hours 58 prisoners had been disarmed and sent to the rear. For the men of J Coy. this was an occasion for satisfaction, since many of their number had been with NP 8901 and had been forced to surrender after the fighting of 2/3 April. Mt. Harriet yielded more than 300 prisoners in all, as well as documents, and equipment including a battlefield radar which had not even been uncrated. This attack, which stands as a model of prior planning and imaginative leadership, cost 42 Cdo. only one dead and 13 wounded.

The attack on Two Sisters by 45 Cdo. was also a classic of its kind. While Y, Z and HQ Coys. went for the eastern peak, X Coy. made a more direct attack on the western peak. By day the two peaks covered a sloping, open area of rough grass; it was over this that the companies moved under cover of darkness on the night of the 11th. X Coy. were slightly late in reaching their objective, so the CO of

45 Cdo. ordered Y and Z Coys. forward at 0430 hrs. It was a silent attack, though the Marines knew that they would have the support of 105s and NGS as well as their own 81mm mortars. Z Coy. was only 250 yards from the Argentine position when a sentry threw a hand illuminant. In the words of 2nd Lt. Paul Mansell of Z Coy.: 'This was ideal for our purposes, for not only did it warn us, but it also confirmed the location of two important fire trenches.' In the assault the Marines used their 84mm Carl Gustav and 66mm LAW anti-tank weapons. The fire-fight lasted about two and a half hours; Lt. Mansell was to recall: '8 Troop had proved that the pusser's flanking attack does work. If only the DS had been there[1] . . .'

[1] Translation: 'Pusser's' = anything which is Service issue; by the book. 'DS' = Directing Staff of an exercise.

Lt.Col. N. F. Vaux (second from right, in beret, cradling SLR), with men of L Coy. of his 42 Cdo. RM, before the advance across East Falkland to Stanley. L Coy. were flown to Mount Challenger when 42 Cdo. seized Mount Kent and other features close to Stanley. Two men are wearing the reversible green/white waterproof smock.

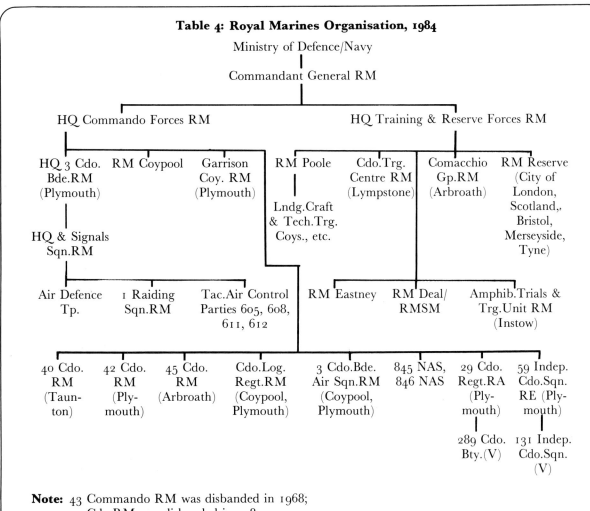

Table 4: Royal Marines Organisation, 1984

Ministry of Defence/Navy

Commandant General RM

HQ Commando Forces RM — HQ Training & Reserve Forces RM

HQ 3 Cdo. Bde.RM (Plymouth) — RM Coypool — Garrison Coy. RM (Plymouth) — RM Poole — Cdo.Trg. Centre RM (Lympstone) — Comacchio Gp.RM (Arbroath) — RM Reserve (City of London, Scotland, Bristol, Merseyside, Tyne)

HQ & Signals Sqn.RM

Lndg.Craft & Tech.Trg. Coys., etc.

Air Defence Tp. — 1 Raiding Sqn.RM — Tac.Air Control Parties 605, 608, 611, 612 — RM Eastney — RM Deal/ RMSM — Amphib.Trials & Trg.Unit RM (Instow)

40 Cdo. RM (Taunton) — 42 Cdo. RM (Plymouth) — 45 Cdo. RM (Arbroath) — Cdo.Log. Regt.RM (Coypool, Plymouth) — 3 Cdo.Bde. Air Sqn.RM (Coypool, Plymouth) — 845 NAS, 846 NAS — 29 Cdo. Regt.RA (Plymouth) — 59 Indep. Cdo.Sqn. RE (Plymouth)

289 Cdo. Bty.(V) — 131 Indep. Cdo.Sqn. (V)

Note: 43 Commando RM was disbanded in 1968; 41 Cdo.RM was disbanded in 1981.

While Z Coy. were fighting their way on to the eastern feature, X Coy. reached the western peak. Y Coy. then passed over the saddle and cleared the southern slopes. By 0840 hrs Two Sisters was in British hands; 45 Cdo. had suffered four dead and 11 wounded.

Capt. Mike Cole, CO of Z Coy., recalled the hours after the announcement of the Argentine surrender, as 45 Cdo. waited to board the LSL *Sir Percival*: 'Small groups of dirty, tired, happy Marines stood talking; others preferred to sit alone on their Bergens, for the first time able to seriously consider the future.'

The Plates

A1: RM Commando, Cyprus, mid-1950s
A Royal Marine adjusts the tuning of his Mk. 6A mine detector during search operations on Cyprus. His combat dress reminds us that Cyprus can sometimes be very cold—Marines even operated on skis at some points during the anti-EOKA campaign. The green Commando beret bears the one-piece cap badge of the Corps worn by Other Ranks: a lion and crown ('dog and basket') above a globe encircled by laurels, in bronze. Over the 1949-pattern khaki serge battledress he wears the Denison smock more usually associated with Airborne Forces. Short khaki puttees, 'Boots SV' (Sole Vulcanised) and the 1937-pattern webbing belt complete the outfit; the belt is blackened in Royal Marine fashion.

A2: RM Commando, 45 Cdo. RM; Port Said, 1956
A Marine of the unit which was lifted in by helicopter during Operation 'Musketeer' at Suez, 6 November 1956. Against the swirling dust of the LZ he wears goggles—the old Second World War-vintage 'gas goggles' of flimsy cellophane, nick-named 'Rommel goggles' after their most famous wearer. He wears the old dark khaki flannel shirt, renowned for its hairy harshness; and the trousers of the Second World War-vintage denim working suit cut like the serge battledress. The '37 webbing is blackened; a shell dressing is taped to the left shoulder, and the full water-bottle can be seen. A green/brown camouflage face veil is worn as a scarf.

The personal weapon is a Mk.V Sten SMG; and he carries the US M20 3.5in. rocket-launcher in its folded mode. This anti-tank weapon was used during the Suez street fighting for blasting open buildings.

A3: Corporal, RM Commandos, UK, mid-1950s
Everyday temperate climate service dress for the Corps, like the Army, was the khaki serge battledress, which lasted from the Second World War until the early 1960s in various forms. This 1949 pattern is mainly distinguishable by the open notched collar, and the map pocket on the outside of the left leg. The attention paid to 'best BD' sometimes approached a cult; every obscure pleat was tracked down and pressed. The normal British rank chevrons, of white herringbone tape on khaki backing, were traditionally 'blanco'd' solid white in the Royal Marines. Also worn on both sleeves is the red-on-dark-blue shoulder title 'Royal Marines/Commando'. The characteristic black

Royal Marine of 40 Cdo. searches an Argentine PoW at Port Howard on West Falkland. He wears a 'headover', a woollen toque which can be worn either as a balaclava, a neck roll or a hat. (Pete Holdgate)

boot polish applied to webbing in the Corps could be brought to a shine for barracks and parade wear; and Marines were quick to point out that it preserved the webbing, while the Army's khaki-green 'blanco', applied damp, degraded it. This NCO wears the ribbons of the British and United Nations Korean War Medals, and the Naval General Service Medal for service in Malayan waters during the Emergency of the 1950s.

B1: Corporal, RM Commandos, Borneo, early 1960s

Negotiating a simple jungle bridge during the 'Confrontation' with Indonesia, this Marine wears the olive green cellular tropical shirt and OG cotton drill trousers. A length of face veil is looped through the loops in his jungle hat. The British rubber and canvas jungle boots were light and cool, but had a maddeningly short life under jungle conditions. His webbing is of 1944 pattern; the small pack had a useful waterproof lining, but was too small to carry much kit. The loop on the right of the belt, where this NCO has fixed a No.36 grenade, was officially

Marines of 42 Cdo. RM search prisoners after the night action on Mount Harriet; tired faces, and head-to-toe mud, tell some of the story of the hard fighting on the night of 11/12 June 1982. The Marine covering the prisoner wears NBC overboots as protection against the wet and muck of the peaty grassland. Note rank tab—vertical epaulette—on the back of the other Marine's smock. (Pete Holdgate)

to steady the butt of a slung rifle. The Browning automatic 12-bore shotgun was a useful weapon under jungle war conditions, and was usually carried by at least one patrol member. The native *parang* slung on the belt was lighter and more effective than the issue machete, despite being hand-made from old car springs! Rank insignia were seldom worn in action, but small-size solid white tapes were occasionally seen.

B2: Lance-Corporal, RM Commandos, Ship Detachment; Far East, early 1960s

Serving in a boarding party from a Royal Navy warship in Malaysian waters, this Royal Marine wears his Commando beret with Royal Navy No.8 working rig of a blue cotton drill shirt, dark blue trousers and naval working boots ('steaming boots'). On the No.8 shirt rank chevrons were worn in red on black, on the right sleeve only. His '58-pattern green webbing belt order is limited to ammunition pouches and water-bottle. His weapon is a Lanchester Mk.1* SMG, from the ship's armoury; developed during the Second World War, the Lanchester was long retained as the issue SMG in the RN and RAF.

B3: RM Commando, Brunei, 1984

On a training deployment to the Brunei jungle, this Commando wears the current British forces jungle combat dress of polyester-cotton DPM tropical shirt/jacket and trousers, the jacket with a zip front covered by a buttoned fly. A sweat-rag is worn round the head; and he has been lucky enough to acquire US jungle boots, which are superior to the British issue. His '58-pattern webbing equipment can be worn as belt order only, but the shoulder yoke spreads the weight and allows a looser belt, preventing chafing at the waist. The '44-pattern water-bottle remains popular, as its aluminium cup can be used for brewing a 'wet'. A toggle rope and 1944 issue machete—'gollock'—are also carried. The Armalite rifle is standard British forces jungle issue.

C1: RM Commando, 41 Cdo. RM; United Nations duty, Cyprus, 1974

The tropical DPM combat jacket is worn here with green polyester-cotton working trousers, puttees, and the 'boots DMS' (direct moulded sole) which

The remnants of the enemy garrison at Fanning Head, who were picked up by helicopter and passed to 40 Cdo. RM. They have been put through the proper prisoner-handling technique by the Intelligence Cell of 3 Cdo. Bde.RM; searched, blindfolded and isolated, they await transport to a PoW cage.

replaced 'boots SV' after the Aden deployments. He wears the UN Forces pale blue beret and yellow metal badge; and a brassard with the UNO insignia above a small national flag. The SLR is carried without a magazine fitted for these duties on the Green Line dividing Greek and Turkish areas of the island.

C2: Machinegunner, 45 Cdo. RM; Radfan Mountains, 1964

A GPMG gunner plods to his position festooned with GPMG link and smoke grenades and carrying a GS ration pack. The khaki drill tropical combat dress is worn without insignia, under '58-pattern webbing and '44-pattern water-bottles—water resupply was a priority during operations in the parched and desolate terrain of the South Arabian mountains, and up to three bottles might be carried, governed by their weight and the need to carry ammunition and other stores. The harsh limestone ridges of the Aden back-country quickly tore up the Marines' 'boots SV', and they were obliged to adopt the tougher-soled Army 'boots DMS'.

C3: Lieutenant-Colonel RM, HMS Britannia, 1970s

White tropical No.1 dress uniform is worn by this senior officer of Royal Marines for duty aboard the Royal Yacht. The normal RM No.1 service dress cap for officers has a white top, red band, and (here) the gold peak decoration for field officers; on all headgear RM officers wear the Corps badge separated, with a gilt 'dog and basket' above a silver

globe with gilt laurels. The white uniform has a standing collar with Corps 'collar dogs', a crimson sash and heavy gold cord epaulettes; the latter bear ranking, and in this case the Royal Cypher worn by officers who have been appointed equerries to members of the Royal Family replaces the normal 'RM' cypher. The gold aiguillettes are also a mark of an equerry. This officer wears the ribbons of the Naval General Service Medal and the Royal Victorian Order, the latter an award given for personal service to the Royal Family.

D1: Corporal, 41 Cdo. RM, UK, 1980

This Royal Marine wears regulation summer barracks dress: the stone-coloured poly-cotton shirt of the Corps, with the green 'TMLs' ('trousers, men's lightweight') common to the Royal Marines and the Army. The beret tends to be worn fuller in the Corps than in the Army, where a shrunken look is thought smart. The 'stable belt' is in Royal Marine colours, which recall the blue of the Royal Navy, the red of the infantry, the green of the light infantry, and the yellow facings of the original mid-17th century 'Duke of York and Albany's Maritime Regiment of Foot'. All ranks of a Royal Marine Commando wear with Blues, Lovat and shirtsleeve uniforms a lanyard in Commando colour on the right shoulder: 3 Cdo.Bde. HQ, green; 40 Cdo., sky blue; 41 Cdo. (disbanded 1981), yellow; 42 Cdo., white; 43 Cdo. (disbanded 1968), mixed old gold and red, retained by Comacchio Gp.; and 45 Cdo., red. A dark blue lanyard is worn by personnel of HQ Cdo. Forces, and the Cdo. Logistic Regiment.

D2: RM recruit, 1980s

This recruit, practising with the L2A3 Stirling SMG, wears the blue beret with red badge-backing issued to RM personnel who have not passed the Commando course.

D3: MAWren, 1980s

Women of the WRNS are attached to the Corps as office and administrative staff, and these 'Marine Attached WRNS' wear the Corps' cap badge and red backing on WRNS headgear.

D4: Sergeant, RM Commandos, 1980s

Everyday working dress since 1969 is the heavy 'woolly pully', with reinforced shoulders and elbows. This NCO, taking a bearing with a prismatic compass, wears it over the unofficial but popular zipped Norwegian Army shirt, and with the DPM combat cap used by British land forces. In the Royal Marines black woven ranking is worn on the cap, allowing identification even when ranking on the chest- and back-tabs of combat clothing is covered by equipment. On both shoulders he wears the red-on-blue Commando title, and on the right arm only the parachutist's qualification brevet above small black rank chevrons. (Attached Commando trained RN personnel wear a white-on-blue title 'Royal Navy/Commando'.)

D5: Lieutenant, RM Commandos; mess dress, UK, 1980s
The red and blue mess dress is worn with a stiff shirt only for the most formal occasions. The red-piped blue 'field service cap' with the Corps globe-and-laurel badge dates originally from 1897. Ranking is arranged vertically on the lapels, above Corps 'collar dogs', and—where applicable—miniatures of decorations: here, the General Service Medal and the South Atlantic Medal. Obscured on the upper right sleeve is a gold and silver version of the parachutist's brevet, made on a scarlet backing for this order of dress.

E1: Regimental Sergeant Major, RM Commandos, UK, 1980s
In April 1964 the Royal Marines—then issued with the khaki battledress and two sets of 'blues'—received the first examples of the 'Lovat' service dress in place of the BD and one set of blues, retaining the second as No.1 dress. The Lovat uniform resembles British Army khaki service dress, but in this unique shade of green. Badges and buttons are bronze. When necessary—in practice, only for ceremonial duty in cold weather—personnel are temporarily issued with khaki greatcoats (with NCOs' ranking on the forearms); but the Royal Marine mackintosh is in a Lovat shade, with gilt ranking for officers, and white embroidered ranking on the shoulder straps for NCOs.

This WO1 in No.2 dress wears the Commando beret with the separated cap badge common to WO1s and officers; WO2s wear a separated badge but with a gilt instead of a silver globe. Corps 'collar dogs' and 'RM' shoulder titles are worn with the

Capt. J. P. Niblet, DFC, RM of the Brigade Air Squadron, who became the first Royal Marine to receive the Distinguished Flying Cross, for service during the Falklands campaign. The BAS gave invaluable support, moving casualties and stores as well as men to the forward edge of the battle area.

Lovat uniform. As a WO1 this RSM wears, in common with officers, the Sam Browne belt, and the navy blue silk lanyard on the left shoulder. The 'warrant badge' of this rank is worn on the right forearm only. A parachutist's qualification brevet is worn on the right shoulder, in gold and silver. Typical medal ribbons for this rank and date might be the British Empire Medal, General Service Medal, and South Atlantic Medal.

E2: Drum-Major D. Dawson, BEM, Corps Drum-Major RM; RMSM Deal, 1980s
The Corps has always taken great pride in its ceremonial duties, and enjoys a very high reputation for its military music in particular. The No.1 dress uniform is basically the 'blues', dating back to the 1920s; and the white Wolseley-pattern helmet with a brass ball and plate, which has been the Corps' ceremonial headgear since before the First World War. Helmet plates vary from band to band.

The senior drum-major wears a lavishly decorated version of the basic 'blues', with gold lacing in light cavalry style, scarlet facings, broad red trouser-stripes, and Corps collar badges; the four gold chevrons on his right sleeve identify his rank. Note that his decorations are worn in miniature form on the ceremonial crossbelt. Junior musicians wear the standard 'blues' of the Other Ranks, with lyre badges replacing the Corps badges on the standing blue collar, and $\frac{5}{16}$ in. trouser welts.

Civilians who only see Royal Marine bands in this glittering rôle on such occasions as 'Beating Retreat' on Horse Guards Parade, or the Royal Jubilee celebrations, should remember that RM bandsmen have a wartime rôle as well. The RM Commando Forces Band served aboard the SS *Canberra* during the Falklands campaign; they worked as stretcher bearers and first aid parties, and also helped handle stores for resupply of the Commandos ashore, while sharing the danger of enemy air attack with the rest of the brigade.

Men of J Coy., 42 Cdo. RM collect Argentine weapons on the airfield of Port Stanley. This made a great image for Fleet Street commentators, but for the men involved it was cold, boring work. It was in the ranks of J Coy. that the repatriated Marines of NP 8901 returned to the Falklands.

E3: Second Lieutenant, 40 Cdo. RM; UK, 1980s

The white-topped service dress cap with its red band and separated badge is unique to the Corps. The dark blue service dress resembles the Army officer's khaki service dress in cut, with an opened collar bearing Corps badges; gilt ranking and (below the rank of colonel) 'RM' titles on the shoulder straps; and $\frac{1}{4}$ in. red welts on the trouser seams, replaced by broader stripes for colonels and above. Majors and above wear gold embroidery on the cap peak; and on ceremonial occasions wear tight 'overall' trousers over spurred 'Wellington' boots—this last applying also to adjutants and ADCs. Note both the officer's dark blue, and 40 Cdo. light blue lanyards, worn on left and right shoulders respectively.

This ensign wears the lavishly decorated colour belt; and behind him we show the Regimental Colour of 40 Cdo. RM. All Regimental Colours are dark blue and of this basic design, apart from the identifying number, and the cords attached to the staff below the finial. The cords are in mixed gold and Commando colour—here, the sky blue of 40 Commando. Note that 'Gibraltar' is the only battle honour displayed. The Queen's Colour of each Commando is based on a large Union Flag.

F1: Lieutenant, 42 Cdo. RM; Norway, 1984

An officer of K Coy., 42 Cdo. on exercise in Norway, wearing the thin white snow suit over DPM Arctic combat dress; the 'cap CW', with ranking in black embroidery on the front flap; and Arctic mittens. His cross-country skis, universally known as 'Pusser's Planks', are treated with a wax suitable for the snow conditions: soft, or well frozen. On his back this officer carries a Norge pack containing the Clansman section radio. In Feb-

ruary 1984 K Coy, were 'trialling' the new webbing equipment associated with the new SA.80 rifle—'Personal Load Carrying Equipment 80'. The weapon, however, is an Armalite M16 with a 30-round magazine, well camouflaged with white tape—as is the PLCE 80 webbing.

F2: LMG gunner, RM Commandos; East Falkland, May 1982

The basic outfit illustrated is the 'smock, combat, Arctic' and 'trousers, combat, Arctic' in DPM camouflage-finish gaberdine, worn over drab green quilted liners (the 'Mao suit'). The Arctic combat smock has a large, wire-stiffened hood; and on the chest and back are 'vertical epaulettes' to carry ranking slides. This tired but determined 'Royal', his face filthy with ingrained camouflage cream, wears a woollen toque, known in the Corps as a 'headover'; and 'wristlets'—actually, fingerless woollen gloves. His Ski-March boots are covered by Mk.1 leather and canvas snow gaiters. Slung from his '58-pattern webbing are an L1A3 smoke grenade; and the 'Marine-pattern' steel helmet, an odd survival which is in fact the old steel 'pot' worn by Royal Armoured Corps crews during the Second World War, retained by the Royal Navy and Royal Marines with conventional internal fittings. The L4A2 LMG is the 7.62mm descendant of the venerable but reliable Bren gun.

Fixed to the rear of his Arctic rucksack is a lightweight shovel, its blade just visible. A sleeping mat and a reversible green/white waterproof are stuffed under the flap of the pack.

G1: Rigid Raider coxswain, 1 Raiding Sqn. RM; Falklands, May 1982

The extreme danger from exposure is reflected in this coxswain's immersion suit, 'cap CW' worn over a 'headover', civilian ski goggles, and 'contact gloves' worn over woollen wristlets. The gloves have areas of small rubber nipples on the surface, to give a grip when handling metal in Arctic conditions. The lightweight life preserver has a rescue lamp on the left shoulder.

G2: Helicopter pilot, 3 Cdo.Bde. RM Air Sqn.; Falklands, May 1982

Over his olive drab flying overalls this pilot—loading his 9mm Browning sidearm—wears the DPM aircrew jacket. This has zipped breast pockets, zipped integral hood, bellows skirt pockets, and Velcro-fastened cuffs and epaulettes. The 'bone dome' and helicopter crews' life preserver are standard NATO items.

The inset illustration shows the insignia worn on the overalls. Ranking is worn on an epaulette slide; ID tags are fixed to a clip on the front of the overalls; and the BAS squadron badge is worn on the upper right sleeve. Above it, here, is a personal parachute qualification brevet.

G3: Sapper, 59 Independent Cdo.Sqn. RE; Falklands, June 1982

Disarming a Spanish C3B anti-tank mine, this sapper wears the Royal Engineers cap badge on his green Commando beret. The DPM camouflage Arctic windproof combat smock has the wired hood rolled in on itself around the neck. Civilian boots are often acquired as an alternative to service issue. The minefield sign is not a standard NATO pattern, but one of those put up to warn local people—the Argentine garrison left widespread, and often unrecorded minefields close to inhabited areas.

H1: RM Commando sniper, 1980s

This 'human tree' wears a sniper's smock (an oversize DPM combat smock with loops and padding) and loose trousers, the surface covered with 'scrim'— in effect, any netting and hessian rags which will completely break up the outline. DPM

The Army Commando dagger sleeve patch in red on dark blue, worn by men who have served with 3 Cdo.Bde. and returned to the Army—sappers of 59 Independent Sqn. RE, gunners of 29 Cdo.Regt. RA, and specialists from support arms who have served in the Cdo. Logistic Regt. RM.

combat caps treated in the same way, or heavily 'scrimmed' steel helmets, are worn to preference. The weapon is a 7.62mm modification of the old bolt-action Lee Enfield No.4, made by Parker Hale Ltd and designated L4A1, with L1A1 telescope sights. The rifle is almost completely covered with hessian and other camouflage materials.

H2: RM Commando rifleman, 198?

A glance into the near-future: this Marine, in standard DPM combat dress and '58-pattern webbing, is illustrated with two items which will be issued to the Commandos within the next year or two: the SA.80 rifle in 5.56mm calibre; and the new ballistic No.6 Combat Helmet GS, whose Airborne equivalent was worn in the Falklands by some personnel of 2 and 3 Para. It has a fitted cover in DPM cloth.

H3: RM Commando 84mm A/T weapon crew, 1980s

The 84mm Carl Gustav can be fired with either 'iron sights' or, as here, with × 3 optical sights. The crew both wear 'NBC Red order': the charcoal-impregnated cloth suit which allows the body to breathe while protecting it from nuclear fall-out and chemical and biological agents, and the S6 respirator. Both Marines wear '58-pattern webbing; the No.1, in the foreground, displays the rear 'kidney pouches' and the poncho 'bum-roll', and has Carl Gustav spares and cleaning pouches slung round his shoulders. He wears the 'Marine-pattern' helmet; the No.2 wears the standard 1943-pattern steel helmet.

H4: RM Commando, Internal Security order; Northern Ireland, 1980s

The ART riot helmet, with its Makrolon polycarbonate visor, is known as a 'Cromwell'—a perhaps unfortunate coincidence, but not a deliberate provocation, since this is the manufacturer's name. The American M69 fragmentation vest has a late-pattern British protective cover with rubber shoulder-rests for the rifle butt; the riot baton is tucked between the vest and the body. His 'belt order' consists of ammunition pouches, water-bottle, respirator and first field dressing. Note the high 'Northern Ireland' patrol boots, which have slightly padded soles. His SLR, fitted with a SUIT sight, is slung; he carries a Makrolon riot shield, and a Schermuly 38mm riot gun for rubber or 25-grain PVC baton rounds.

Notes sur les planches en couleur

A1 A la recherche de mines posées par les terroristes de l'*EOKA*, ce *Marine* porte la *Denison smock* de parachutiste, modèle deuxième guerre mondiale et les pantalons du *battledress* kaki, modèle 1949. **A2** Atterrissant d'un hélicoptère à Suez, ce *Marine* porte une tenue qui évoque la fin de la deuxième guerre mondiale: chemise en laine épaisse kaki et pantalons dans la version tissu de travail *denim* de la *battledress*. Les Marines royaux noircissaient toujours leur équipement *webbing* modèle 1937. Les armes sont un *Sten* et le lance-roquettes *US 3.5 in*, utilisé à Suez pour démolir les bâtiments lors du combats de rue. **A3** La *battledress*, version 1949, portée comme uniforme quotidien jusqu'en 1964; notez les chevrons de rang blanchis et le *webbing* noirci, particuliers aux *Royal Marines* et le nom d'épaule '*Royal Marines/Commando*' en rouge sur bleu.

B1 En patrouille dans la jungle contre les infiltrateurs indonésiens, il porte une chemise et des pantalons tropicaux vert olive et des bottes de jungle de fabrication britannique de mauvaise qualité. L'équipement de *webbing* est du modèle 1944; les armes sont une grenade No.36, un fusil automatique *Browning*, et un *parang* acquis sur place. **B2** Appartenant à un groupe de débarquement provenant d'un petit navire de guerre en patrouille au large de Bornéo, il porte '*No.8 Working dress*' et un équipement de *webbing* minimal; remarquez les chevrons de rang portés sur cet uniforme. L'arme est le vénérable *Lanchester*, conservé longtemps à bord des navires de la marine. **B3** Uniforme de combat de jungle britannique actuel, porté avec *webbing* de modèle 1958, la gourde bien conçue de 1944 et une machete réglementaire; le fusil *Armalite* est distribué aux troupes britanniques pour opérations de jungle.

C1 Tenue de travail quotidienne de la décennie 1970, avec brassard et béret UNO. **C2** '*Khaki drill*', tenue de combat légère de couleur sable et un chapeau sont portés pour cette campagne dans le désert; l'arme est la mitrailleuse *GPMG*. **C3** *No.1 Dress* tropicale blanche spéciale pour l'officier qui commande les *Marines* à bord du yacht royal, *HMS Britannia*. Les aiguillettes dorées permettent de reconnaître les officiers nommés comme aides-de-camp de sa Majesté.

D1 Tenue quotidienne de caserne pendant l'été. Notez la cordelière jaune du *41 Cdo*; sur la chemise et la tunique vert *Lovat*, le *40 Cdo* porte une cordelière bleu pâle, le *42 Cdo* une cordelière blanche et le *45 Cdo* une cordelière écarlate. La '*stable belt*' est dans les couleurs des *Royal Marines*. **D2** Les hommes qui n'ont pas encore effectué la formation de *Commando* portent ce béret. **D3** Coiffe des WRNS attachés au corps. **D4** Coiffe de combat camouflée avec chevrons de rang de *sergeant*, qui se retrouvent sur la manche du pullover de travail sous '*Commando*' *title* et les '*ailes*' de parachutiste. **D5** Tenue de mess avec la chemise empesée portée pour les évènements très difficiles, le vieux '*field service cap*', l'insigne de rang sur les revers et les '*ailes*' de parachutiste sur l'épaule droite.

E1 Uniforme de service vert *Lovat* porté depuis 1964. Ce *Warrant Officer* supérieur porte ses insignes de rang sur l'avant-bras droit seulement ainsi que la ceinture d'épée du modèle officier. Les officiers et WOs portent tous la cordelière bleu foncé sur l'épaule gauche. **E2** *No.1 dress* tenue somptueusement décorée d'un chef d'orchestre; la musique militaire et de cérémonie a toujours été un accomplissement dont le Corps est particulièrement fier. **E3** Modèle pour officier de la *No.1 dress*, portée par un porte-drapeau, avec la coiffe *No.1 dress* d'officier. La *Regimental Colour* (arriere-plan) est la même pour tous les *Commandos*, à part l'inscription, mais les cordons sont dans la couleur de la cordelière de l'unité.

F1 Tenue de camouflage pour l'Arctique, skis de cross-country et fusil Armalite; le *webbing* est le modèle expérimental pour le nouveau fusil SA.80, qui vient d'être mis en service. **F2** Le *Marine* lourdement chargé de la campagne des Malouines, portant la mitrailleuse légère et fiable *Bren*. La toque en laine s'appelle un '*headover*' dans le Corps.

G1 'Tenue de plongée' et veste de sauvetage sont essentielles pour les équipages des bateaux d'assaut légers en hiver. **G2** La version pour aviateurs de la veste *DPM* est portée par dessus une combinaison de vol. **G3** Ce '*sapper*', enlevant les mines des argentins après leur défaite, porte une tenue camouflée d'Arctique, comme à F2.

H1 Camouflage typique de tireur isolé; les *Royal Marines* ont la meilleure formation comme tireurs des forces britanniques. **H2** Le nouveau casque No.6, mis en service et le fusil SA.80 de 5,56 mm. **H3** Equipage de lance-roquettes, 84mm Carl Gustav dans tenues '*NBC*' (nucléaires, biologiques, chimiques) et le *webbing* de modèle 1958. **H4** Marine en tenue de 'sécurité intérieure': casque d'émeutes, bouclier, gourdin et fusil tirant des balles en plastique; '*flak jacket*'.

Farbtafeln

A1 Dieser *Marine* sucht nach Minen von *EOKA*-Terroristen und trägt den *Denison Smock* eines Fallschirmjägers mit dem Muster aus dem 2. Weltkrieg und eine Hose der khakifarbenen *battledress* nach einem Muster von 1949. **A2** Dieser *Marine* landet mit einem Hubschrauber bei Suez und trägt eine Uniform, die an das Ende des 2. Weltkrieges erinnert: ein schweres, khakifarbenes Wollhemd und eine Hose aus *Denim*, eine Arbeitsversion der *battledress*. Die Royal Marines schwärzten ihre *Webbing*-Ausrüstung von 1937 immer an. Die Waffen sind ein *Sten* sowie ein *US3, 5in* Raketenwerfer, der bei Suez in Strassengefechten zum Aufsprengen von Gebäuden verwendet wurde. **A3** Die *Battledress* von 1949, die bis 1964 als Uniform für jeden Tag galt. Beachten Sie die weissen Rangwinkel und das angeschwärzte *Webbing*, das für die *Royal Marines* eigentümlich war, sowie den rot-auf-blauen Schulter-*Title* der *Royal Marines/Commando*.

B1 Auf einer Dschungelpatrouille gegen indonesische Eindringlinge trägt dieser Soldat ein olivgrünes Tropenhemd mit Hose und britische Dschungelstiefel schlechter Qualität. Die *Webbing*-Ausrüstung stammt von 1944. Die Waffen sind eine Granate Nr.36, ein automatisches *Browning*-Gewehr und ein lokal gekauftes *Parang*. **B2** Dieser Soldat gehört zu einem Landungstrupp von einem kleinen Kriegsschiff vor Borneo und trägt eine *No.8 Working Dress* mit minimaler *Webbing*-Ausrüstung. Beachten Sie die roten und schwarzen Rangwinkel auf dieser Uniform. Die Waffe ist eine der berühmten *Lanchester*, die es noch lange an Bord von Marineschiffen gab. **B3** Die derzeitige britische Dschungel-Kampfuniform mit 1958er *Webbing*, einer robusten Wasserflasche von 1944 und einer Machete. Das *Armalite*-Gewehr wird für den Dschungeleinsatz an britische Truppen ausgegeben.

C1 Die Arbeitsuniform für jeden Tag aus den 70er Jahren mit UNO-Felduniformmütze und Armbinde. **C2** Leichte, sandfarbene '*Khaki Drill*' Kampfuniform und Mütze für Wüsteneinsätze. Die Waffe ist ein *GPMG*-Maschinengewehr. **C3** Weisse Tropenausrüstung der *No.1 Dress* für den Offizier, der für die *Marines* an Bord der königlichen Jacht *HMS Britannia* verantwortlich ist. Die goldenen Aiguilletten kennzeichnen Offiziere, die zu Adjutanten Ihrer Majestät ernannt wurden.

D1 Sommer-Kasernenuniform für jeden Tag. Beachten Sie die gelbe Kordel des *41 Cdo*. Auf dem Hemd und dem *Lovat*-grünen Waffenrock tragen die *40 Cdo*. eine hellblaue Kordel, die *42 Cdo*. eine weisse und die *45 Cdo*. eine scharlachrote. Der *Stable Belt* hat die Farben der Royal Marines. **D2** Soldaten, die den *Commando*-Kurs noch nicht hinter sich haben, tragen diese Felduniformmütze. **D3** Kopfbedeckung der WRNS, die zum Korps gehören. **D4** Getarnte Kampfmütze mit Rangwinkel eines *Sergeants*, die auf dem Ärmel des Arbeitspullovers unter dem *Commando Title* und den 'Flügeln' des Fallschirmspringers nochmals auftauchen. **D5** Messeuniform mit steifem Hemd für sehr formelle Veranstaltungen sowie der alten '*field service cap*', Ranginsignien auf dem Revers und 'Flügel' des Fallschirmjägers auf der rechten Schulter.

E1 Seit 1964 wurde die *Lovat*-grüne Dienstuniform getragen. Dieser ranghöhere *Warrant Officer* trägt seine Ranginsignien nur am rechten Unterarm. Er trägt ausserdem ein Offiziersdegenkoppel. Alle Offiziere und *WOs* haben eine dunkelblaue Kordel an der linken Schulter. **E2** Die reichlich mit Orden versehene *No.1 Dress* eines Kapellmeisters. Auf Fest- und Militärmusik war das Korps immer besonders stolz. **E3** Die Offiziersausführung der blauen *No.1 Dress*, mit der hier ein Fahnenträger bekleidet ist; er trägt auch die *No.1 Dress*-Mütze des Offiziers. Die *Regimental Colour* (im Hintergrund) ist dieselbe mit Ausnahme der Buchstaben-bezeichnung aller *Commandos*, die herunterhängenden Schnüre haben dieselben Farben wie die Kordeln der Einheit.

F1 Arktische Tarnbekleidung, Gelände-Ski und Armalite-Gewehr. Das *Webbing* ist ein Experiment für das neue SA.80-Gewehr, das gerade erst eingeführt wird. **F2** Der schwerbeladene *Marine* im Falkland-Krieg trägt das 7,62 mm Ausführung des zuverlässigen, leichten *Bren*-Maschinengewehrs. Die Wolltoque wird innerhalb des Korps als '*Headover*' bezeichnet.

G1 Im Winter sind für die Besatzung leichter Landungsfahrzeuge Taucheranzüge und Schwimmwesten notwendig. **G2** Man trägt die Fliegerversion der *DPM*-Jacke über dem Overall. **G3** Dieser '*Sapper*', der nach der Kapitulation argentinische Minen entfernt, trägt, wie F2 eine arktische Tarnausrüstung.

H1 Typische Tarnung eines Scharfschützen. In der britischen Armee haben die *Royal Marines* die beste Scharfschützenausbildung. **H2** Der neue Nr.6 Helm, der gerade eingeführt wird, und das 5,56 mm Gewehr SA.80. **H3** Eine Raketenwerfermannschaft mit einem 84mm Carl Gustav in '*NBC*'-Anzügen (ABC; atomar, biologisch, chemisch) und *Webbing* von 1958. **H4** Ein *Marine* in 'interner Sicherheitsuniform': Strassenkampfhelm, Schild, Schlagstock und Gewehr mit Plastikkugeln sowie '*flak jacket*'.